DISNEY'S

KiM POSSIBLE

VOLUME 6

©Disney

SERIES CREATED BY
BOB SCHOOLEY AND MARK McCORKLE

TOKYOPOP®

LOS ANGELES • TOKYO • LONDON

Contributing Editors - Gregg Schaufeld & Amy Court Kaemon
Copy Editor - Carol Fox & Aaron Sparrow
Graphic Design & Lettering - Rob Steen
Graphic Artists - Jennifer Nunn-Iwai & Tomás Montalvo-Lagos
Cover Layout - Patrick Hook

Editor - Elizabeth Hurchalla
Managing Editor - Jill Freshney
Production Coordinator - Antonio DePietro
Production Manager - Jennifer Miller
Art Director - Matt Alford
Editorial Director - Jeremy Ross
VP of Production - Ron Klamert
President & C.O.O. - John Parker
Publisher & C.E.O. - Stuart Levy

Come visit us online at www.TOKYOPOP.com

A ☺**TOKYOPOP**® Cine-Manga™

TOKYOPOP Inc.
5900 Wilshire Blvd., Suite 2000, Los Angeles, CA 90036

Kim Possible Volume 6
© 2003 Disney Enterprises, Inc.

ISBN: 1-59182-569-5
First TOKYOPOP printing: May 2004

10 9 8 7 6 5 4 3 2 1

Printed in China

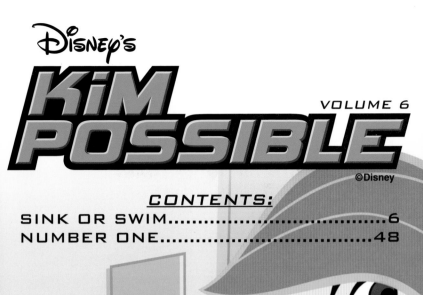

DISNEY's
KiM POSSIBLE

VOLUME 6

©Disney

CONTENTS:

SINK OR SWIM.......................................6
NUMBER ONE....................................48

CHARACTER BIOS

KIM POSSIBLE

A STUDENT AT MIDDLETON HIGH SCHOOL WHO LOVES CHEERLEADING, SHOPPING AND HANGING OUT WITH HER BEST FRIEND, RON. BUT KIM'S NO ORDINARY GIRL—SHE CAN DO ANYTHING, INCLUDING SAVING THE WORLD IN HER SPARE TIME.

RON STOPPABLE

KIM'S BEST FRIEND AND SIDEKICK.

RUFUS

RON'S PET NAKED MOLE RAT.

WADE

THE 10-YEAR-OLD GENIUS WHO RUNS KIM'S WEBSITE AND KEEPS HER UPDATED ON EVIL SCHEME DEVELOPMENTS.

BONNIE

KIM'S BIGGEST RIVAL ON THE MIDDLETON HIGH CHEER SQUAD.

MR. BARKIN

KIM'S PERMANENT SUBSTITUTE TEACHER.

GILL

A FORMER CAMPER AT CAMP WANNAWEEP—NOW A GENETICALLY MUTATED FISH-BOY.

WILL DU

A TEEN AGENT WORKING FOR THE GLOBAL JUSTICE NETWORK.

DUFF KILLIGAN

AN EX-PROFESSIONAL GOLFER WITH A TERRIBLE TEMPER. BANNED FROM EVERY GOLF COURSE IN THE WORLD.

PROF. SYLVAN GREEN

A FORMER WEAPONS EXPERT, NOW AN AVID GARDENER.

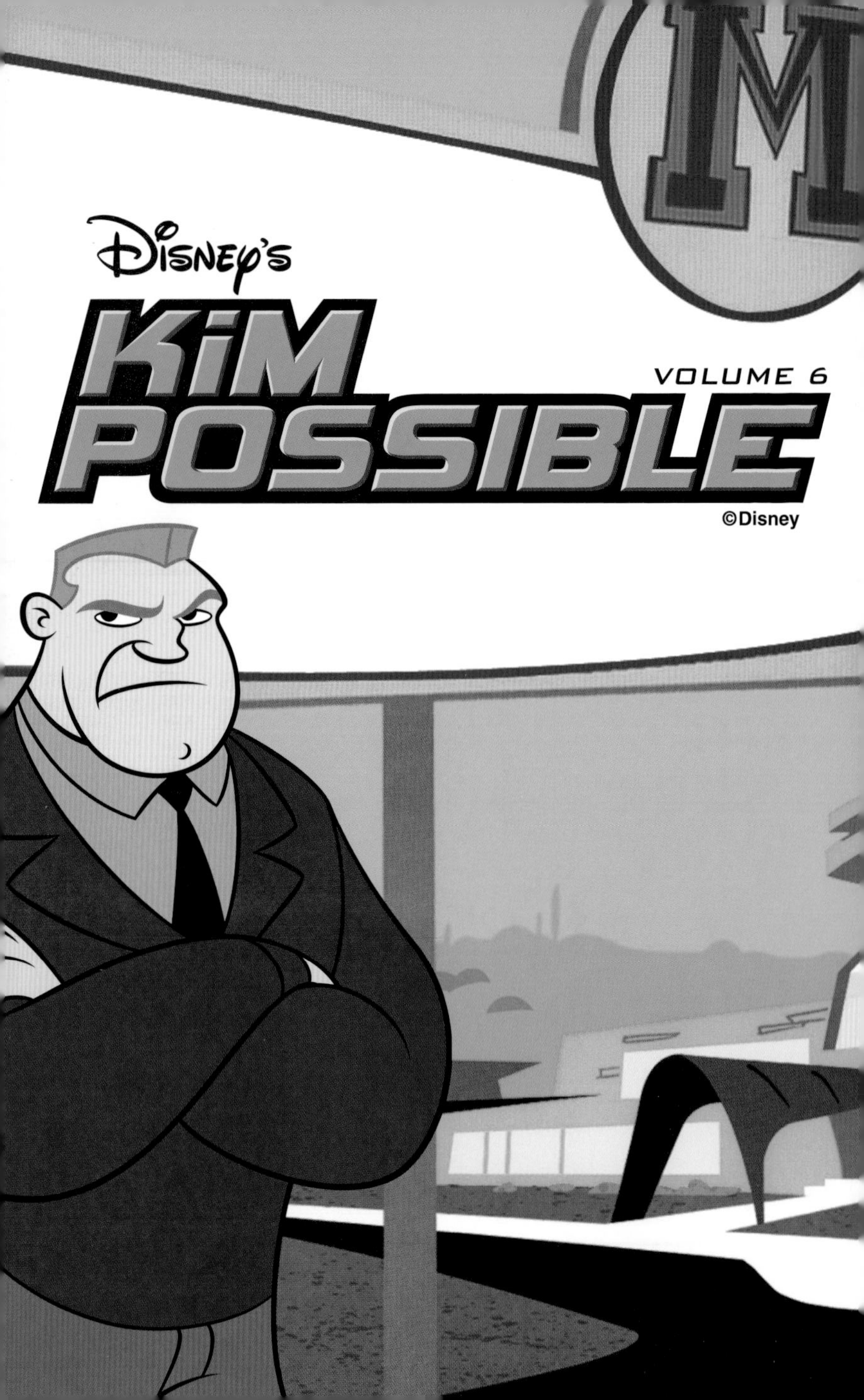
Disney's
KIM POSSIBLE
VOLUME 6
©Disney

Episode 11: Sink or Swim

Kim's bus breaks down on the way to a cheerleading competition, leaving the entire squad stranded at Camp Wannaweep. And when a monstrous fish-boy begins to pick off the team one by one, a surprising hero emerges from the fray.

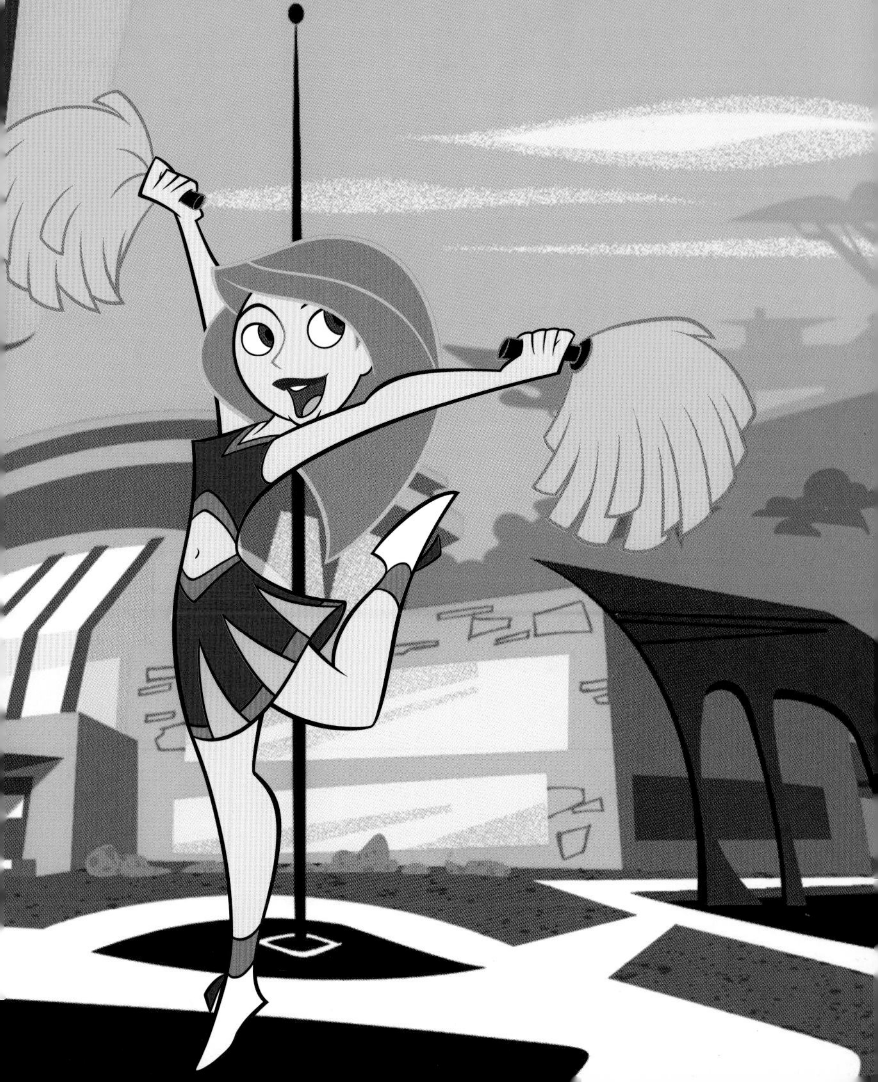

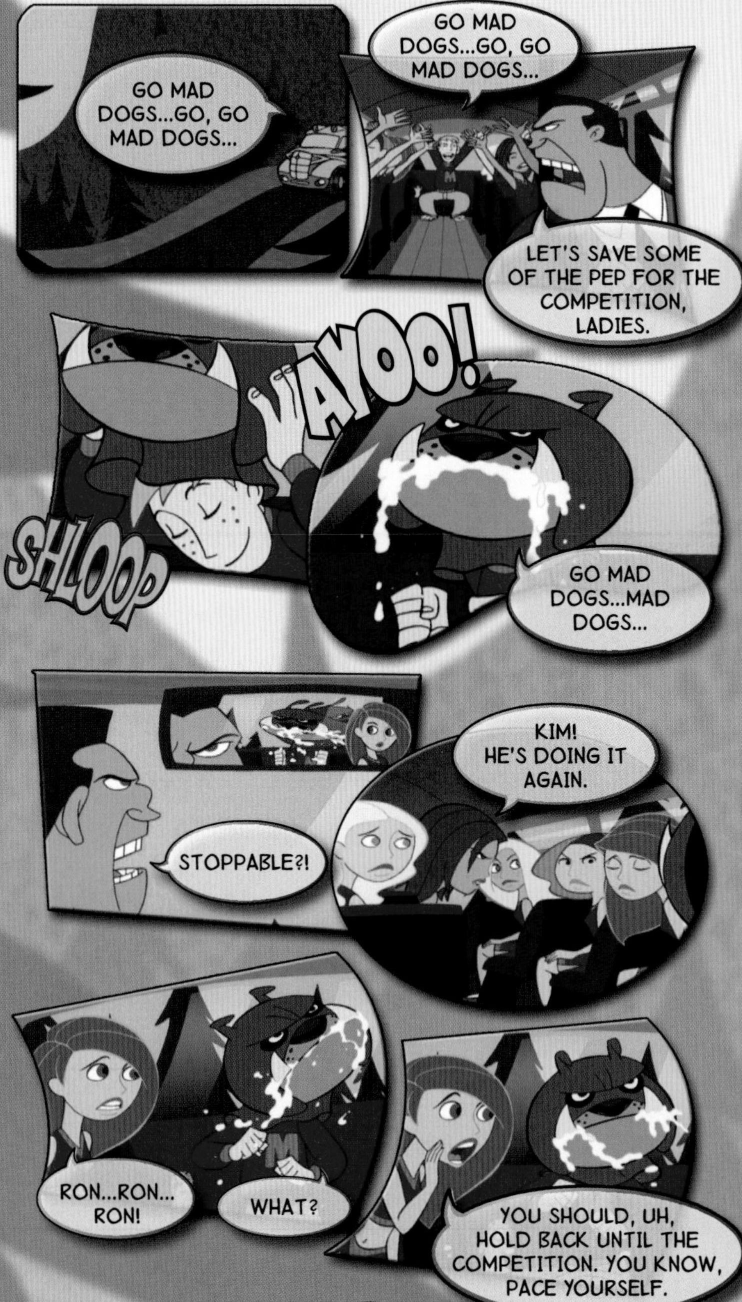
GO MAD DOGS...GO, GO MAD DOGS...
GO MAD DOGS...GO, GO MAD DOGS...
LET'S SAVE SOME OF THE PEP FOR THE COMPETITION, LADIES.
YAYOO!
SHLOOP
GO MAD DOGS...MAD DOGS...
STOPPABLE?!
KIM! HE'S DOING IT AGAIN.
RON...RON... RON!
WHAT?
YOU SHOULD, UH, HOLD BACK UNTIL THE COMPETITION. YOU KNOW, PACE YOURSELF.

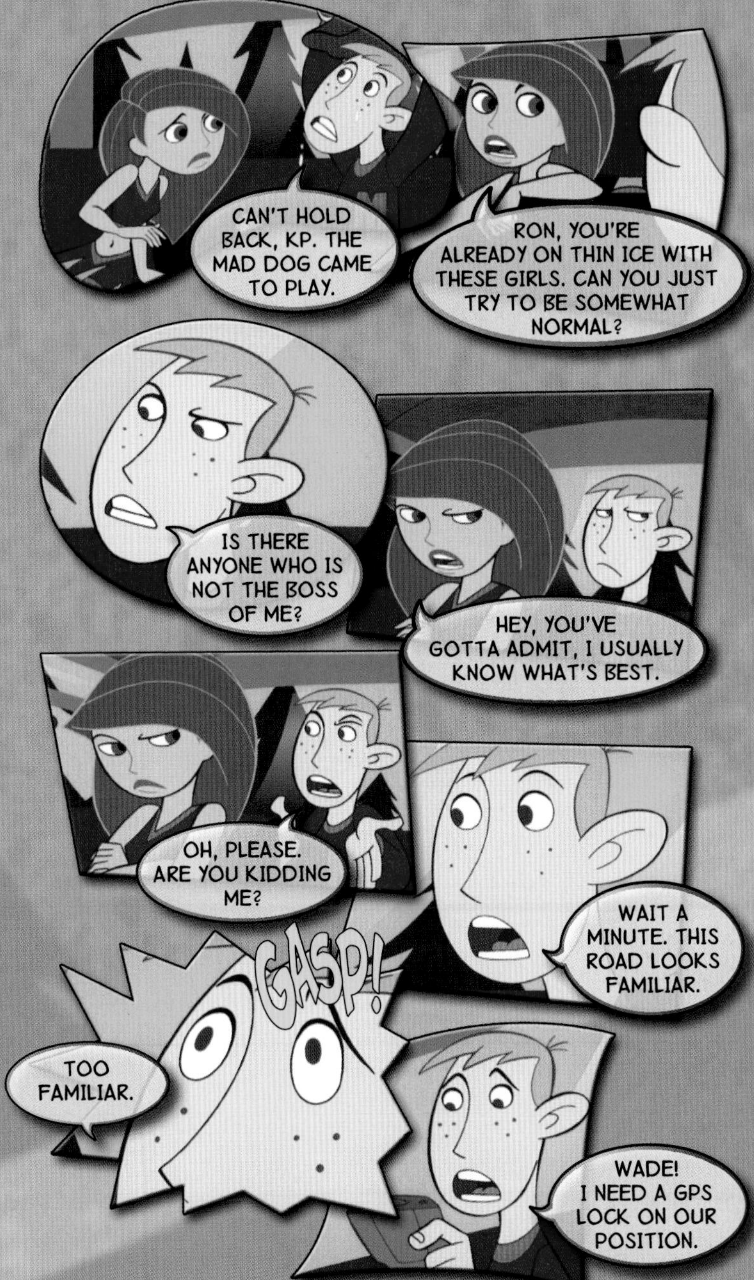
CAN'T HOLD BACK, KP. THE MAD DOG CAME TO PLAY.
RON, YOU'RE ALREADY ON THIN ICE WITH THESE GIRLS. CAN YOU JUST TRY TO BE SOMEWHAT NORMAL?
IS THERE ANYONE WHO IS NOT THE BOSS OF ME?
HEY, YOU'VE GOTTA ADMIT, I USUALLY KNOW WHAT'S BEST.
OH, PLEASE. ARE YOU KIDDING ME?
WAIT A MINUTE. THIS ROAD LOOKS FAMILIAR.
GASP!
TOO FAMILIAR.
WADE! I NEED A GPS LOCK ON OUR POSITION.

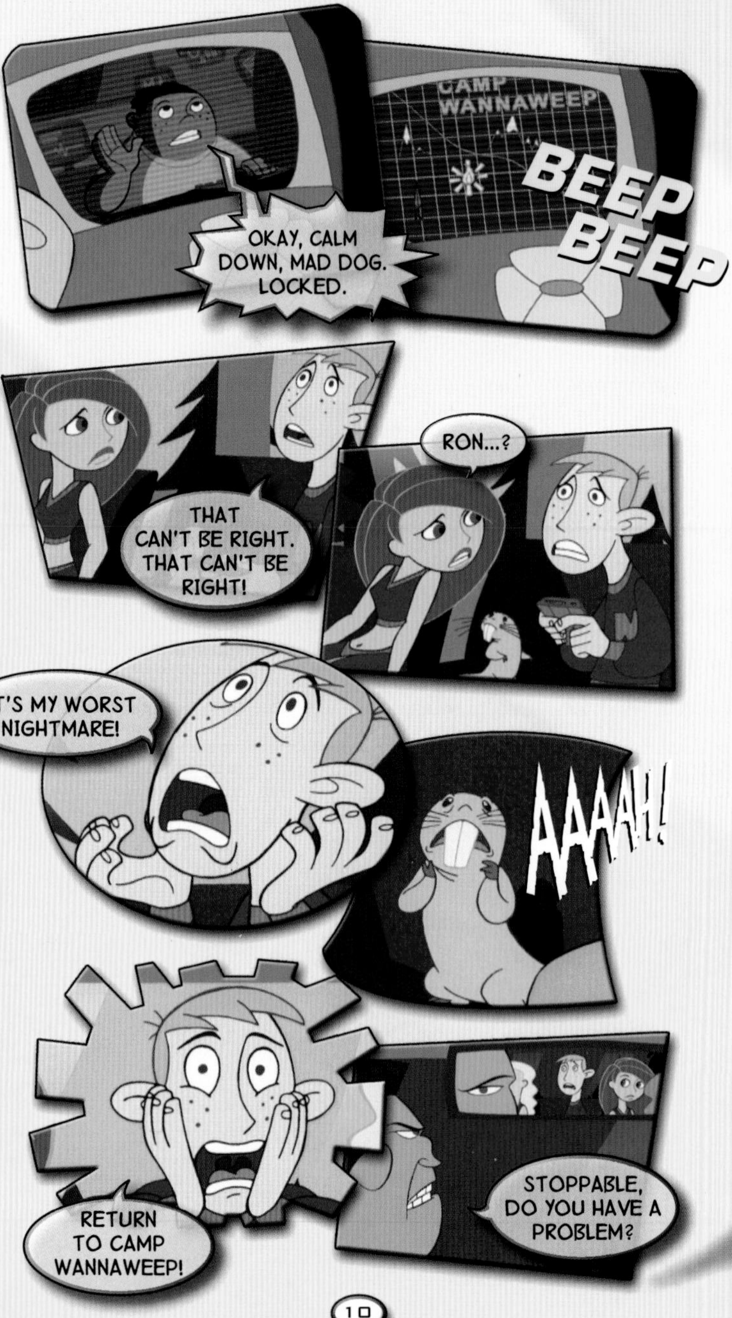
OKAY, CALM DOWN, MAD DOG. LOCKED.
CAMP WANNAWEEP
BEEP BEEP
THAT CAN'T BE RIGHT. THAT CAN'T BE RIGHT!
RON...?
IT'S MY WORST NIGHTMARE!
AAAAH!
RETURN TO CAMP WANNAWEEP!
STOPPABLE, DO YOU HAVE A PROBLEM?

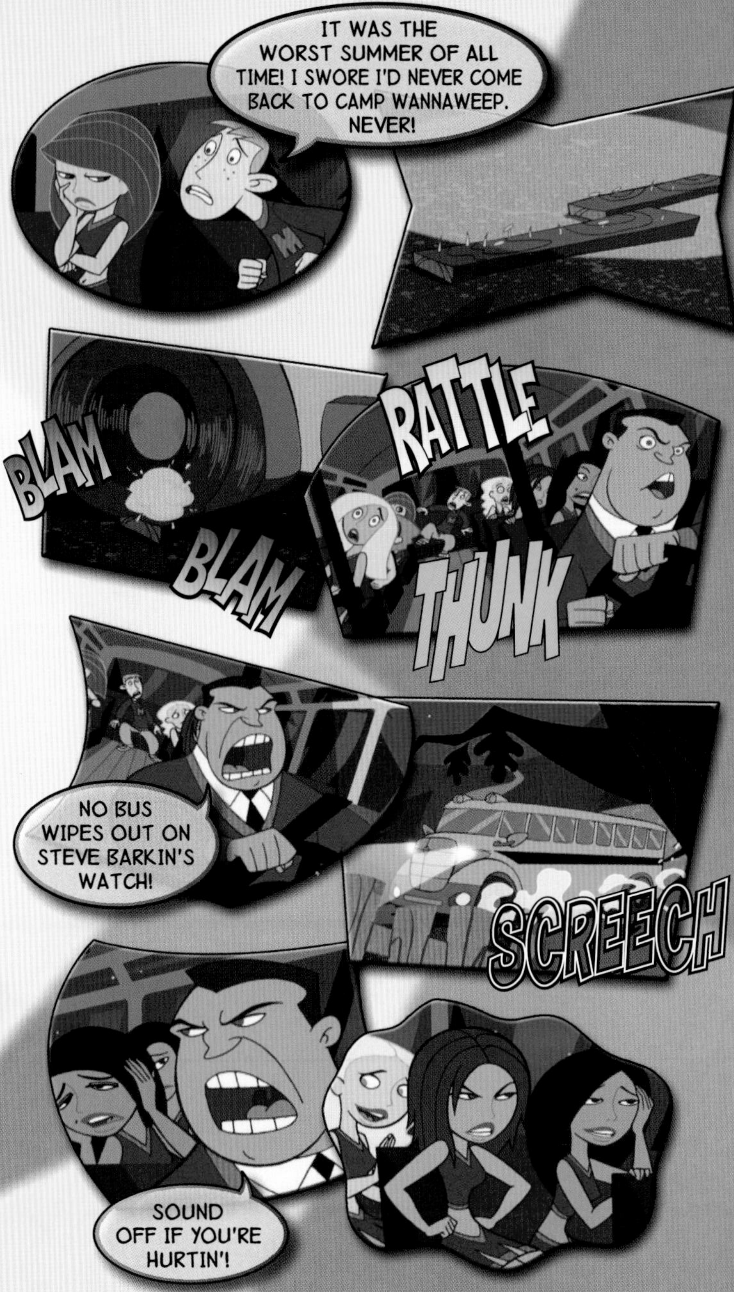
IT WAS THE WORST SUMMER OF ALL TIME! I SWORE I'D NEVER COME BACK TO CAMP WANNAWEEP. NEVER!
BLAM
BLAM
RATTLE
THUNK
NO BUS WIPES OUT ON STEVE BARKIN'S WATCH!
SCREECH
SOUND OFF IF YOU'RE HURTIN'!

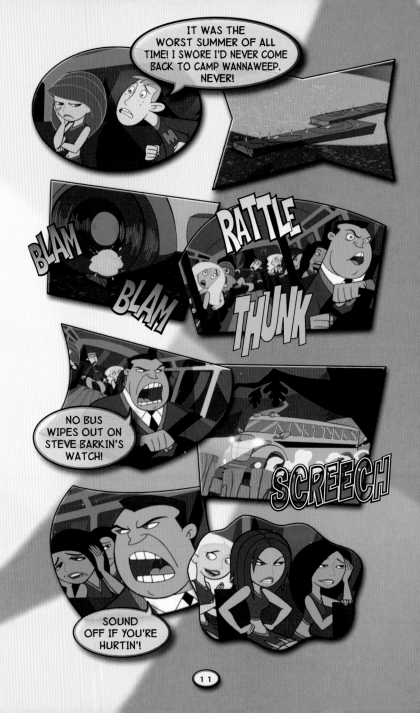

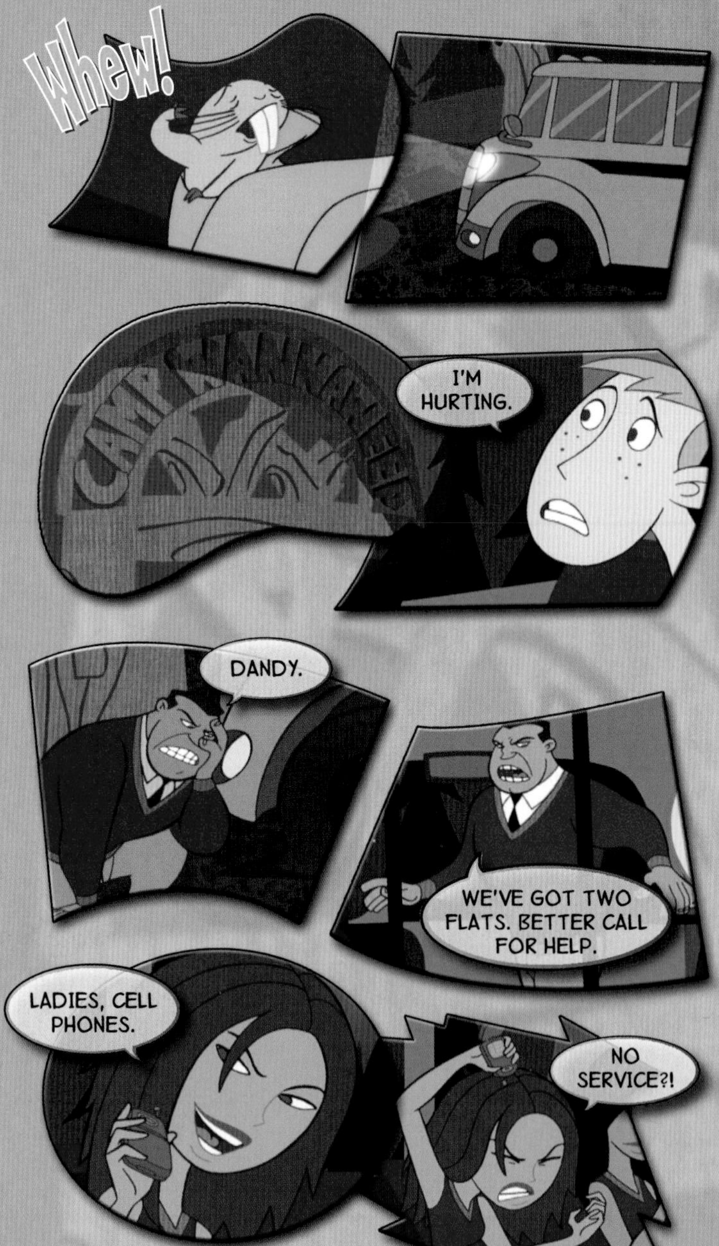
Whew!
I'M HURTING.
DANDY.
WE'VE GOT TWO FLATS. BETTER CALL FOR HELP.
LADIES, CELL PHONES.
NO SERVICE?!

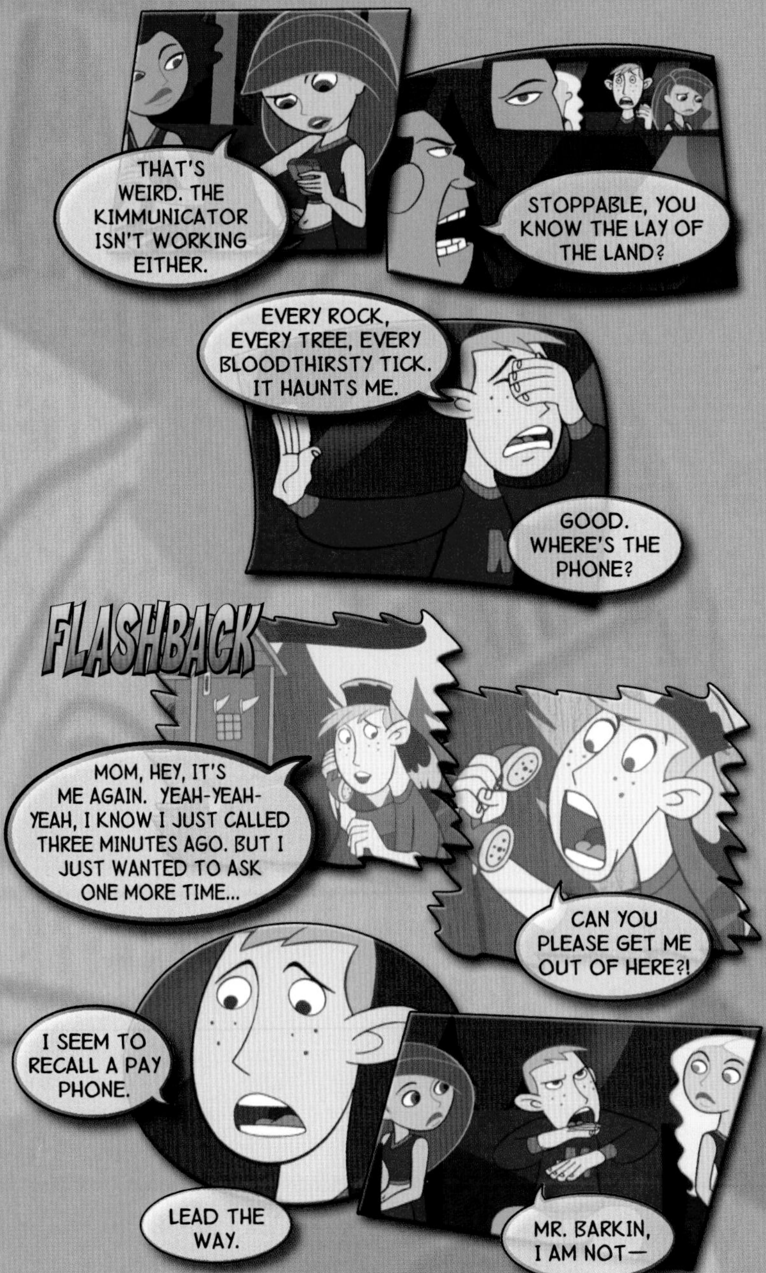
THAT'S WEIRD. THE KIMMUNICATOR ISN'T WORKING EITHER.
STOPPABLE, YOU KNOW THE LAY OF THE LAND?
EVERY ROCK, EVERY TREE, EVERY BLOODTHIRSTY TICK. IT HAUNTS ME.
GOOD. WHERE'S THE PHONE?
FLASHBACK
MOM, HEY, IT'S ME AGAIN. YEAH-YEAH-YEAH, I KNOW I JUST CALLED THREE MINUTES AGO. BUT I JUST WANTED TO ASK ONE MORE TIME...
CAN YOU PLEASE GET ME OUT OF HERE?!
I SEEM TO RECALL A PAY PHONE.
LEAD THE WAY.
MR. BARKIN, I AM NOT—

WHAT DID YOU SAY?

I SAID, LEAD THE WAY.

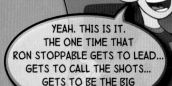

RON, PLEASE JUST TAKE US TO THE PAY PHONE.

YEAH. THIS IS IT. THE ONE TIME THAT RON STOPPABLE GETS TO LEAD... GETS TO CALL THE SHOTS... GETS TO BE THE BIG BOSS MAN.

OH, I WILL. BUT YOU NEED TO UNDERSTAND THIS: I AM YOUR ONLY HOPE.

WHAT? RON, NORMAL.

LISTEN UP, PEOPLE! CAMP WANNAWEEP IS A DANGEROUS AND WICKED PLACE. AND AMONG US, ONLY I, RON STOPPABLE, KNOW HOW TO SURVIVE HERE.

OH NO!

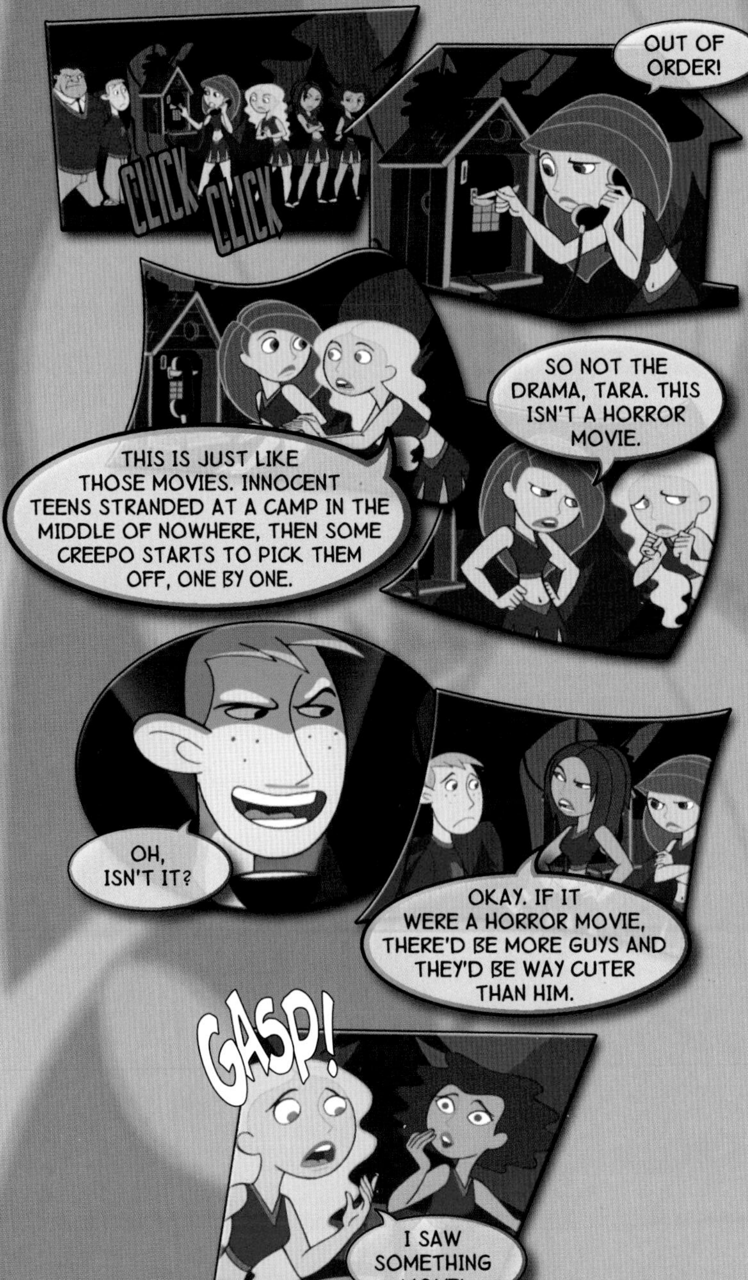
CLICK CLICK
OUT OF ORDER!
THIS IS JUST LIKE THOSE MOVIES. INNOCENT TEENS STRANDED AT A CAMP IN THE MIDDLE OF NOWHERE, THEN SOME CREEPO STARTS TO PICK THEM OFF, ONE BY ONE.
SO NOT THE DRAMA, TARA. THIS ISN'T A HORROR MOVIE.
OH, ISN'T IT?
OKAY. IF IT WERE A HORROR MOVIE, THERE'D BE MORE GUYS AND THEY'D BE WAY CUTER THAN HIM.
GASP!
I SAW SOMETHING MOVE!

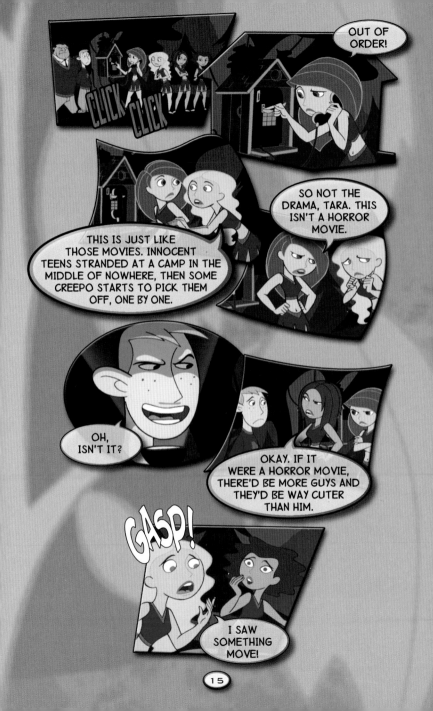

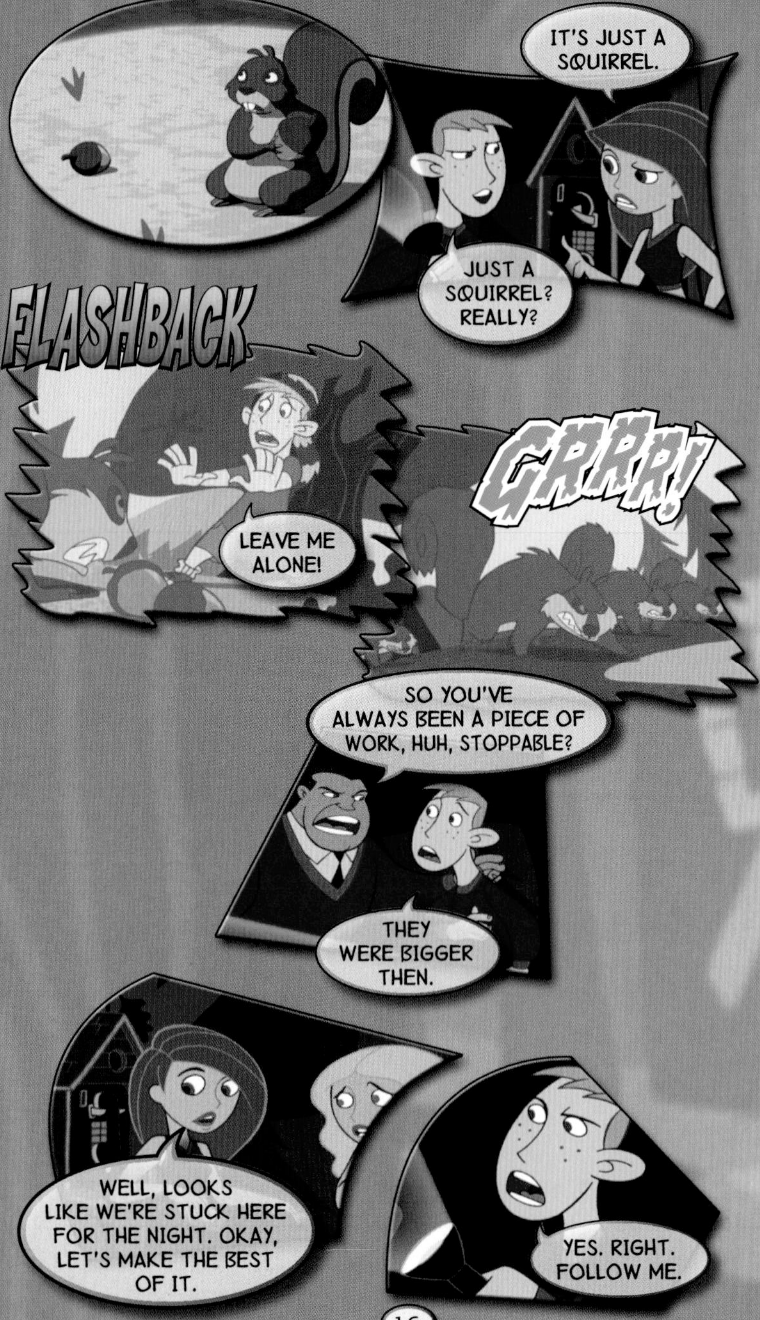
IT'S JUST A SQUIRREL.
JUST A SQUIRREL? REALLY?
FLASHBACK
LEAVE ME ALONE!
GRRR!
SO YOU'VE ALWAYS BEEN A PIECE OF WORK, HUH, STOPPABLE?
THEY WERE BIGGER THEN.
WELL, LOOKS LIKE WE'RE STUCK HERE FOR THE NIGHT. OKAY, LET'S MAKE THE BEST OF IT.
YES. RIGHT. FOLLOW ME.

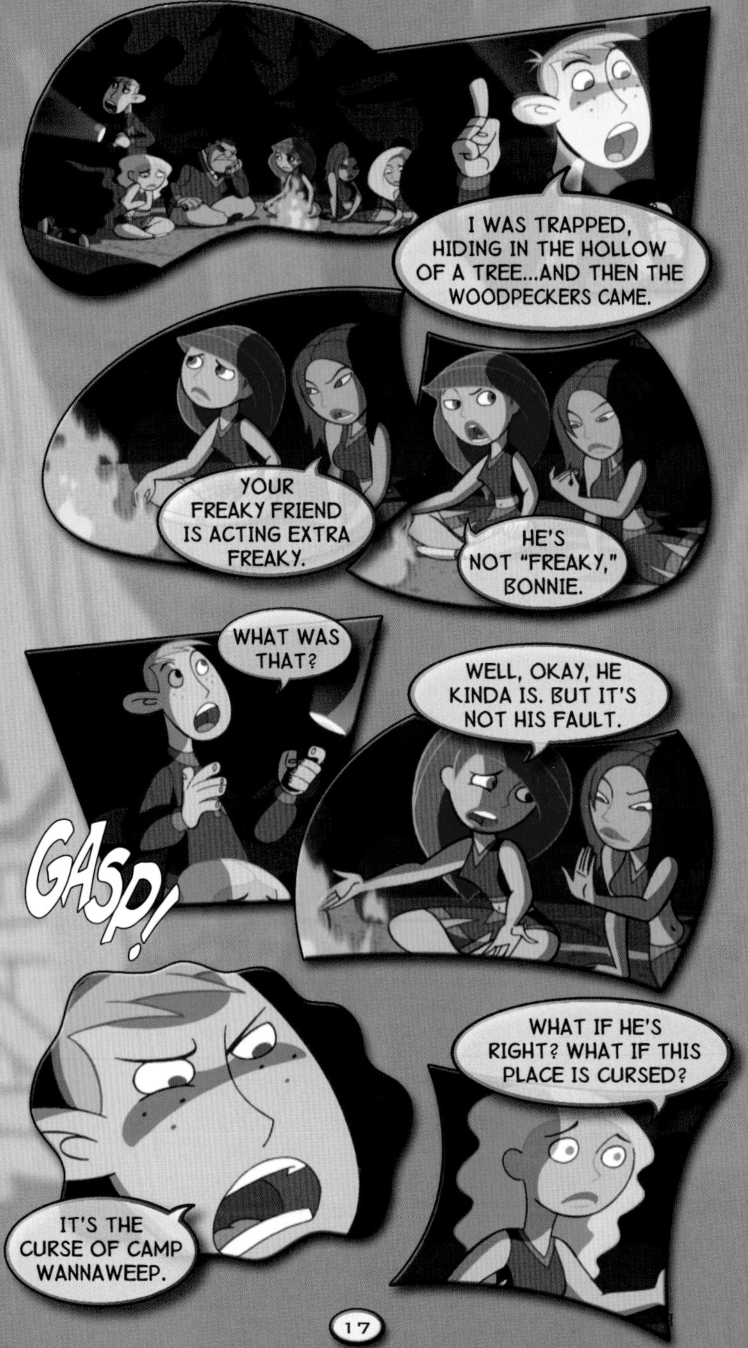
I WAS TRAPPED, HIDING IN THE HOLLOW OF A TREE...AND THEN THE WOODPECKERS CAME.
YOUR FREAKY FRIEND IS ACTING EXTRA FREAKY.
HE'S NOT "FREAKY," BONNIE.
WHAT WAS THAT?
WELL, OKAY, HE KINDA IS. BUT IT'S NOT HIS FAULT.
GASP!
IT'S THE CURSE OF CAMP WANNAWEEP.
WHAT IF HE'S RIGHT? WHAT IF THIS PLACE IS CURSED?

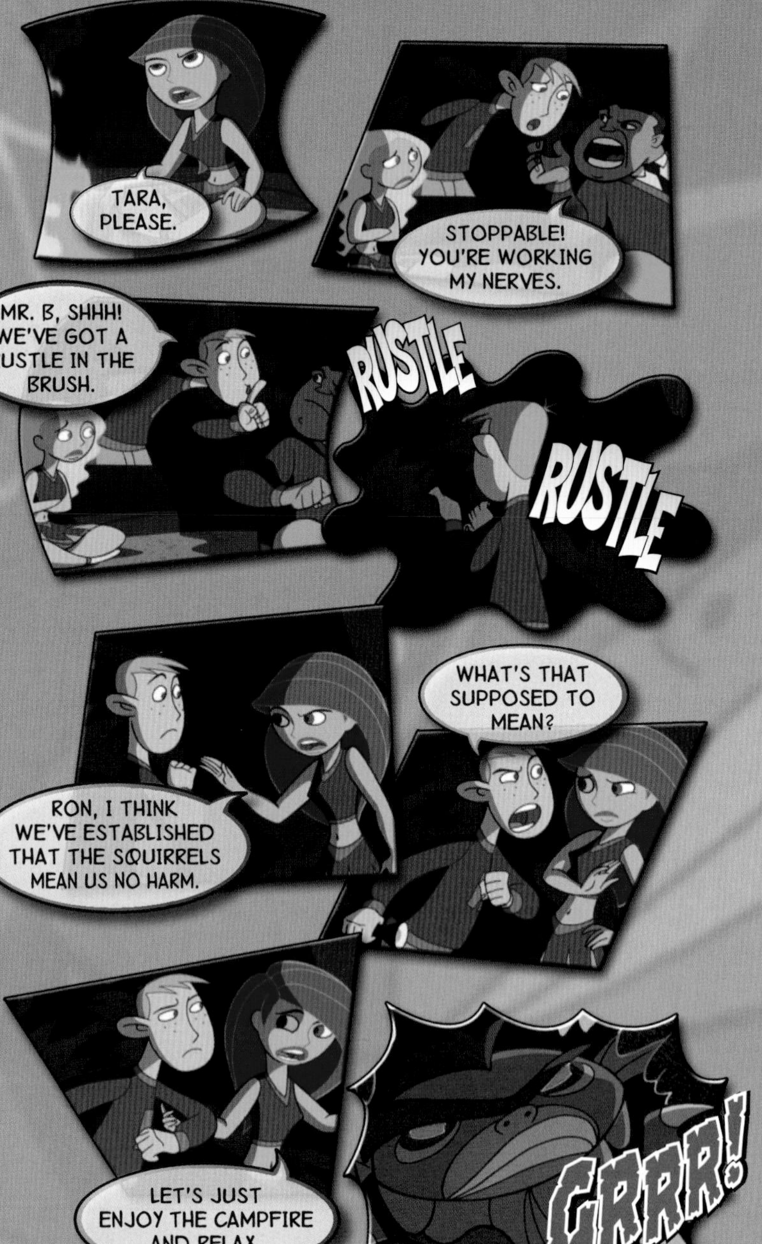
TARA, PLEASE.
STOPPABLE! YOU'RE WORKING MY NERVES.
MR. B, SHHH! WE'VE GOT A RUSTLE IN THE BRUSH.
RUSTLE
RUSTLE
RON, I THINK WE'VE ESTABLISHED THAT THE SQUIRRELS MEAN US NO HARM.
WHAT'S THAT SUPPOSED TO MEAN?
LET'S JUST ENJOY THE CAMPFIRE AND RELAX.
GRRR!

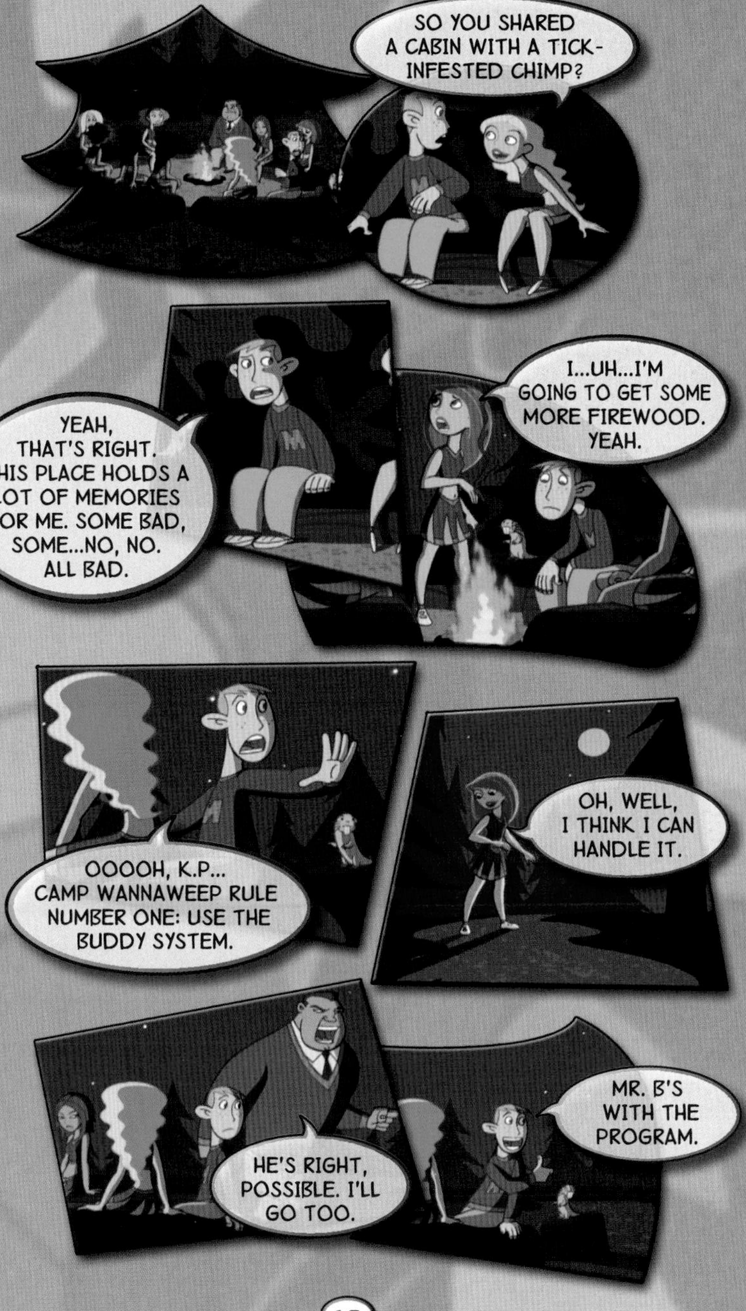
SO YOU SHARED A CABIN WITH A TICK-INFESTED CHIMP?
YEAH, THAT'S RIGHT. THIS PLACE HOLDS A LOT OF MEMORIES FOR ME. SOME BAD, SOME...NO, NO. ALL BAD.
I...UH...I'M GOING TO GET SOME MORE FIREWOOD. YEAH.
OOOOH, K.P... CAMP WANNAWEEP RULE NUMBER ONE: USE THE BUDDY SYSTEM.
OH, WELL, I THINK I CAN HANDLE IT.
HE'S RIGHT, POSSIBLE. I'LL GO TOO.
MR. B'S WITH THE PROGRAM.

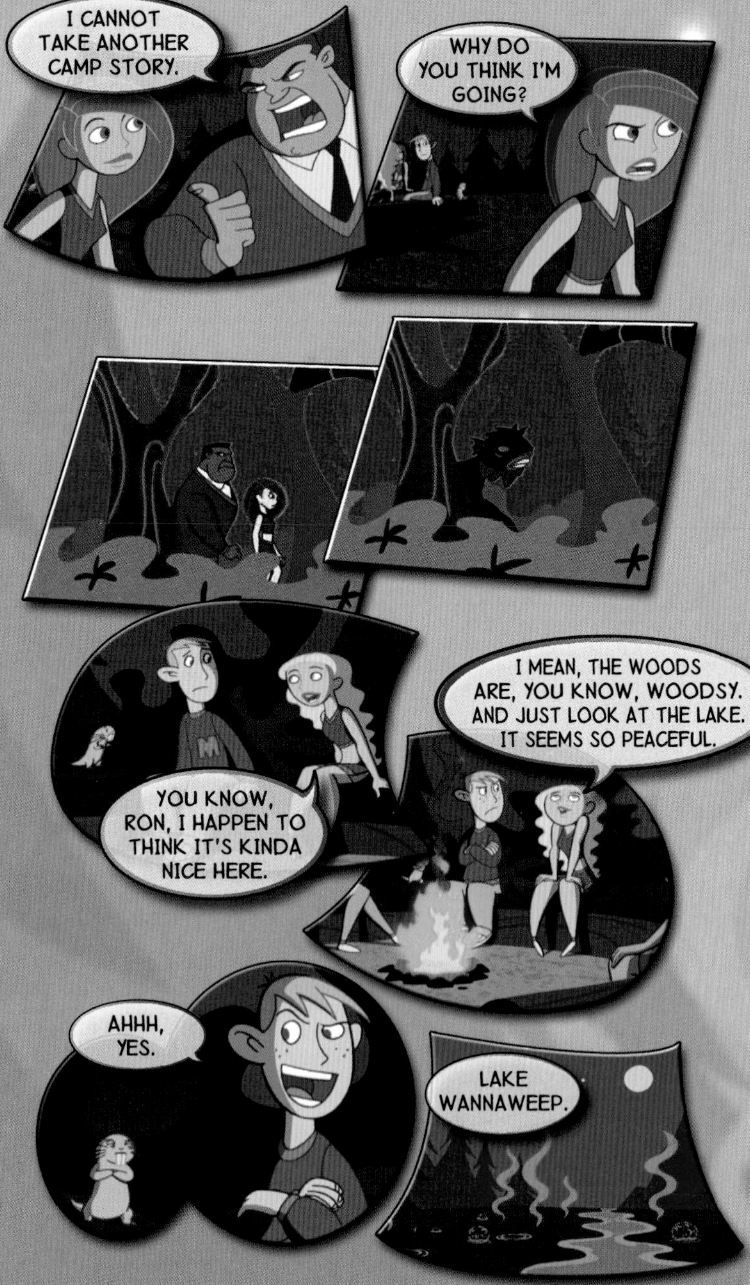
I CANNOT TAKE ANOTHER CAMP STORY.
WHY DO YOU THINK I'M GOING?
YOU KNOW, RON, I HAPPEN TO THINK IT'S KINDA NICE HERE.
I MEAN, THE WOODS ARE, YOU KNOW, WOODSY. AND JUST LOOK AT THE LAKE. IT SEEMS SO PEACEFUL.
AHHH, YES.
LAKE WANNAWEEP.

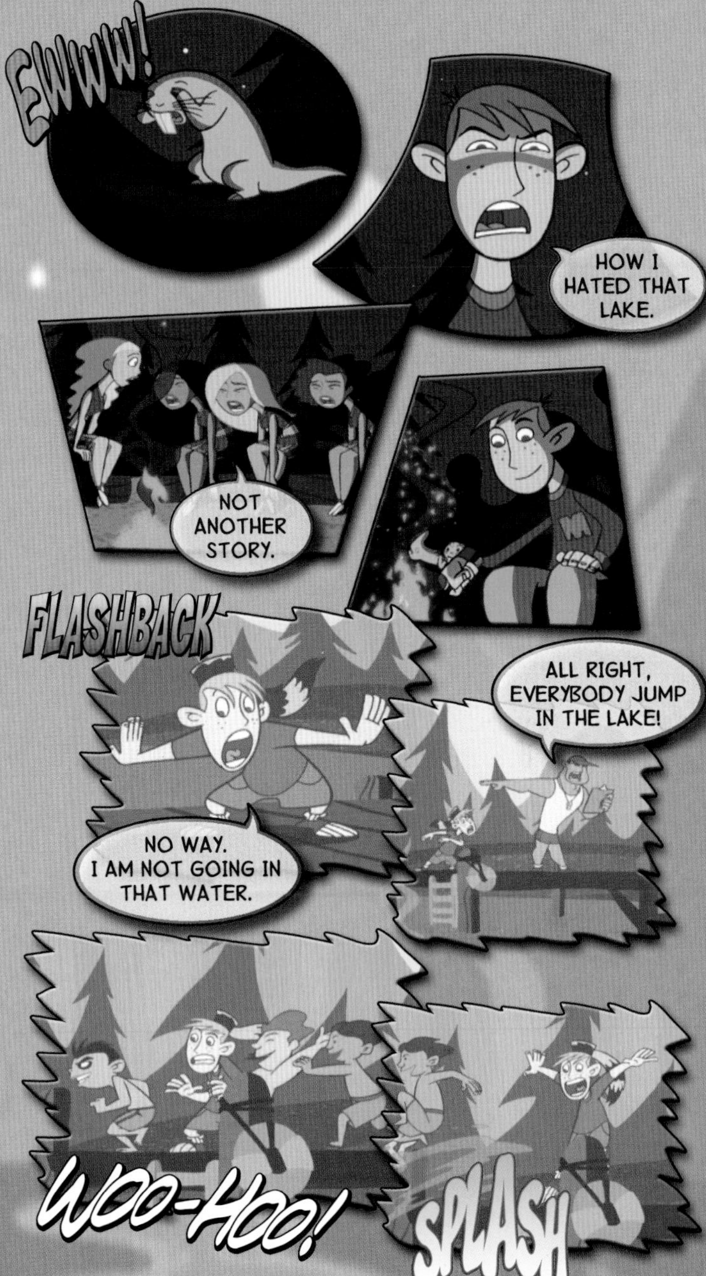
EWWW!
HOW I HATED THAT LAKE.
NOT ANOTHER STORY.
FLASHBACK
ALL RIGHT, EVERYBODY JUMP IN THE LAKE!
NO WAY. I AM NOT GOING IN THAT WATER.
WOO-HOO!
SPLASH

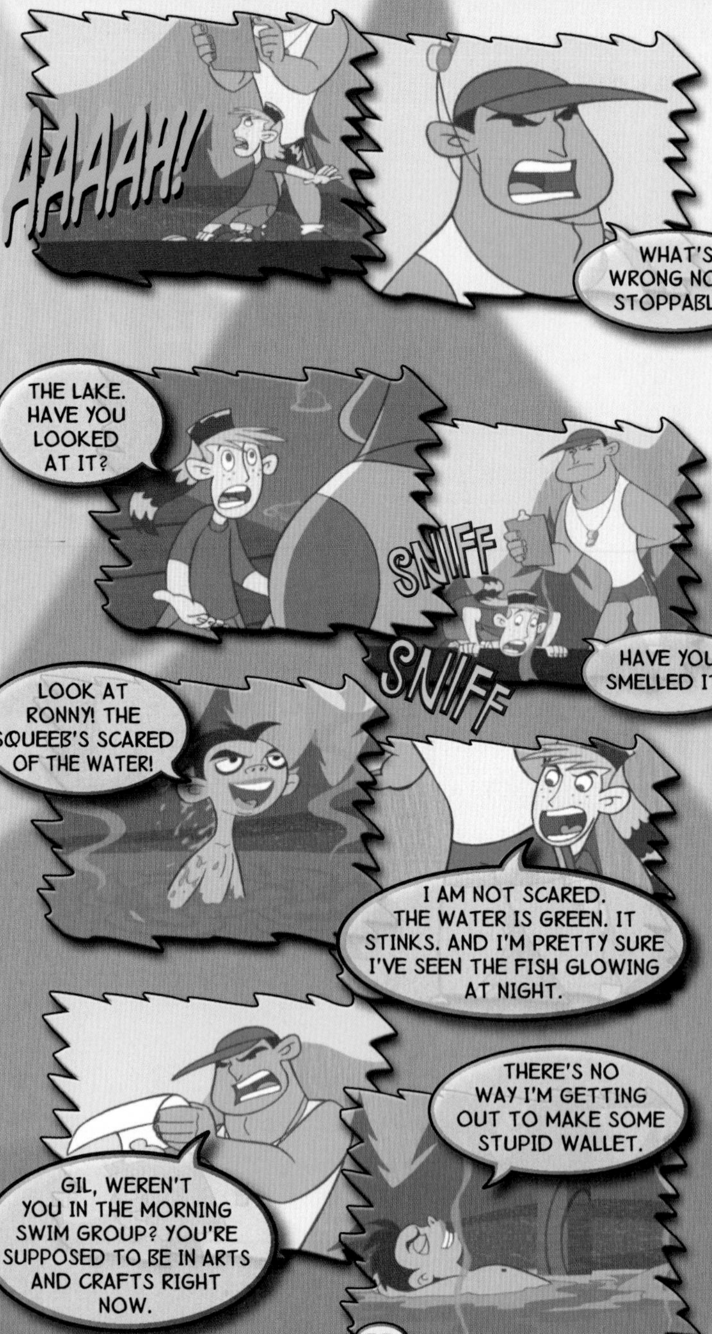
AAAAH!
WHAT'S WRONG NOW, STOPPABLE?
THE LAKE. HAVE YOU LOOKED AT IT?
SNIFF
SNIFF
HAVE YOU SMELLED IT?
LOOK AT RONNY! THE SQUEEB'S SCARED OF THE WATER!
I AM NOT SCARED. THE WATER IS GREEN. IT STINKS. AND I'M PRETTY SURE I'VE SEEN THE FISH GLOWING AT NIGHT.
GIL, WEREN'T YOU IN THE MORNING SWIM GROUP? YOU'RE SUPPOSED TO BE IN ARTS AND CRAFTS RIGHT NOW.
THERE'S NO WAY I'M GETTING OUT TO MAKE SOME STUPID WALLET.

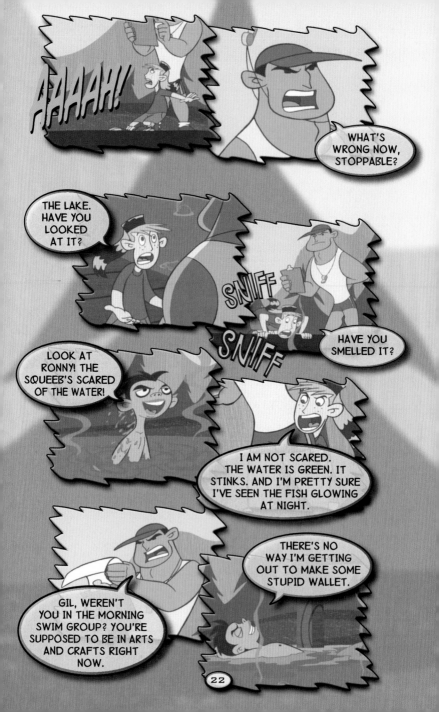

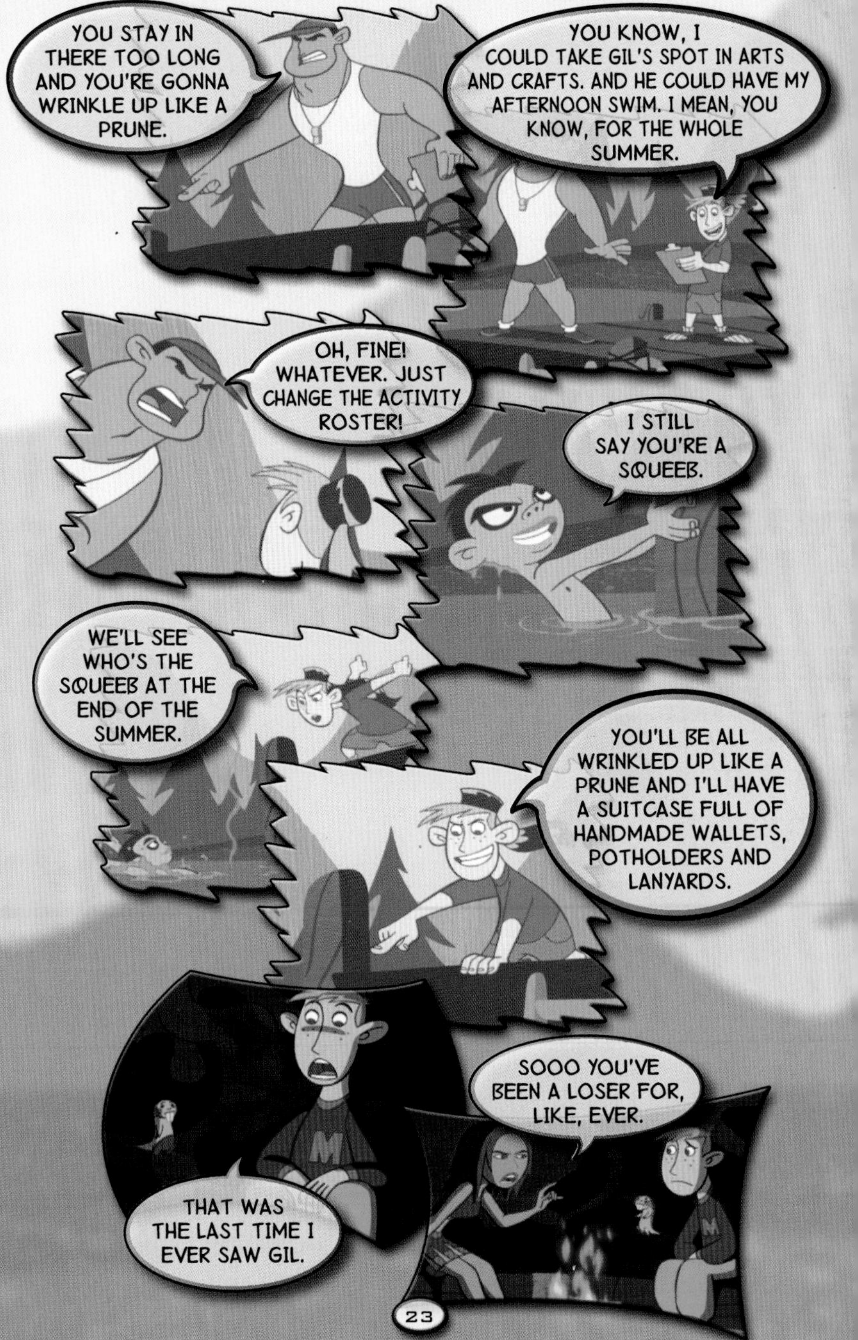
YOU STAY IN THERE TOO LONG AND YOU'RE GONNA WRINKLE UP LIKE A PRUNE.
YOU KNOW, I COULD TAKE GIL'S SPOT IN ARTS AND CRAFTS. AND HE COULD HAVE MY AFTERNOON SWIM. I MEAN, YOU KNOW, FOR THE WHOLE SUMMER.
OH, FINE! WHATEVER. JUST CHANGE THE ACTIVITY ROSTER!
I STILL SAY YOU'RE A SQUEEB.
WE'LL SEE WHO'S THE SQUEEB AT THE END OF THE SUMMER.
YOU'LL BE ALL WRINKLED UP LIKE A PRUNE AND I'LL HAVE A SUITCASE FULL OF HANDMADE WALLETS, POTHOLDERS AND LANYARDS.
THAT WAS THE LAST TIME I EVER SAW GIL.
SOOO YOU'VE BEEN A LOSER FOR, LIKE, EVER.

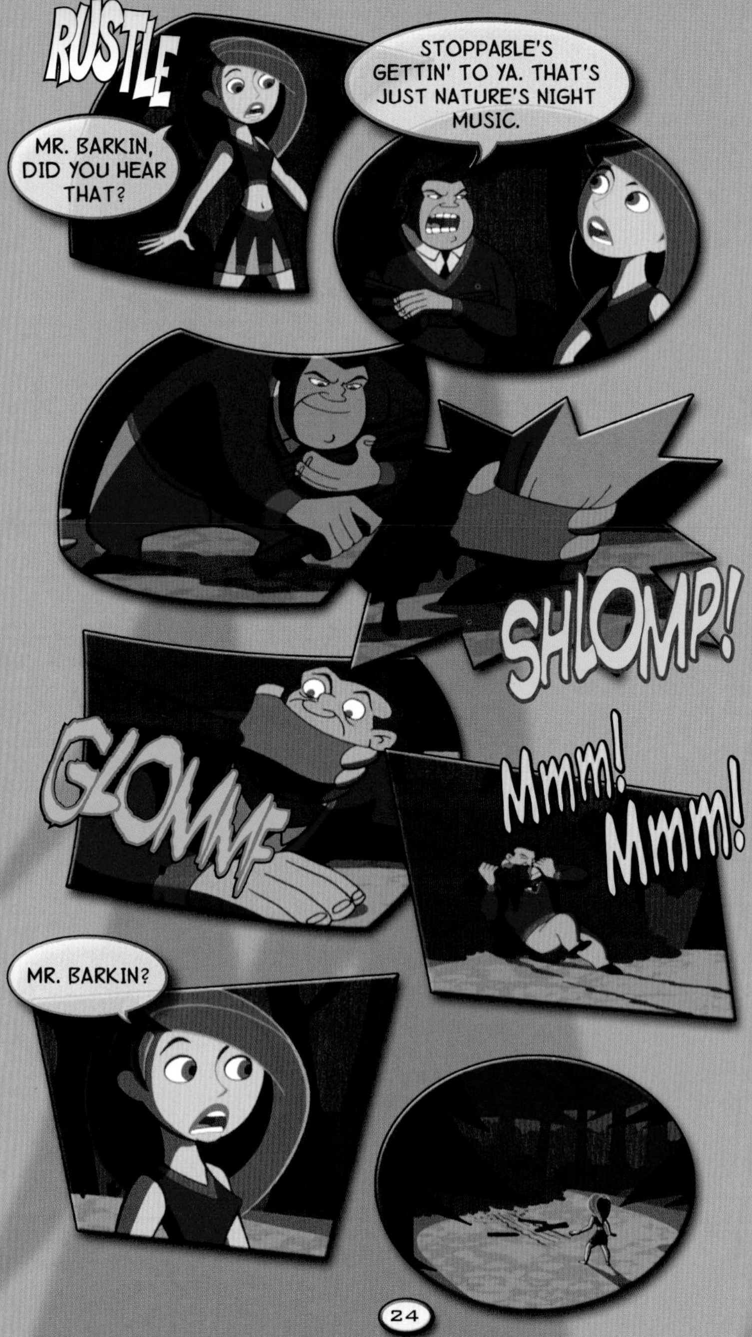
RUSTLE
MR. BARKIN, DID YOU HEAR THAT?
STOPPABLE'S GETTIN' TO YA. THAT'S JUST NATURE'S NIGHT MUSIC.
SHLOMP!
GLOMMF
Mmm! Mmm!
MR. BARKIN?

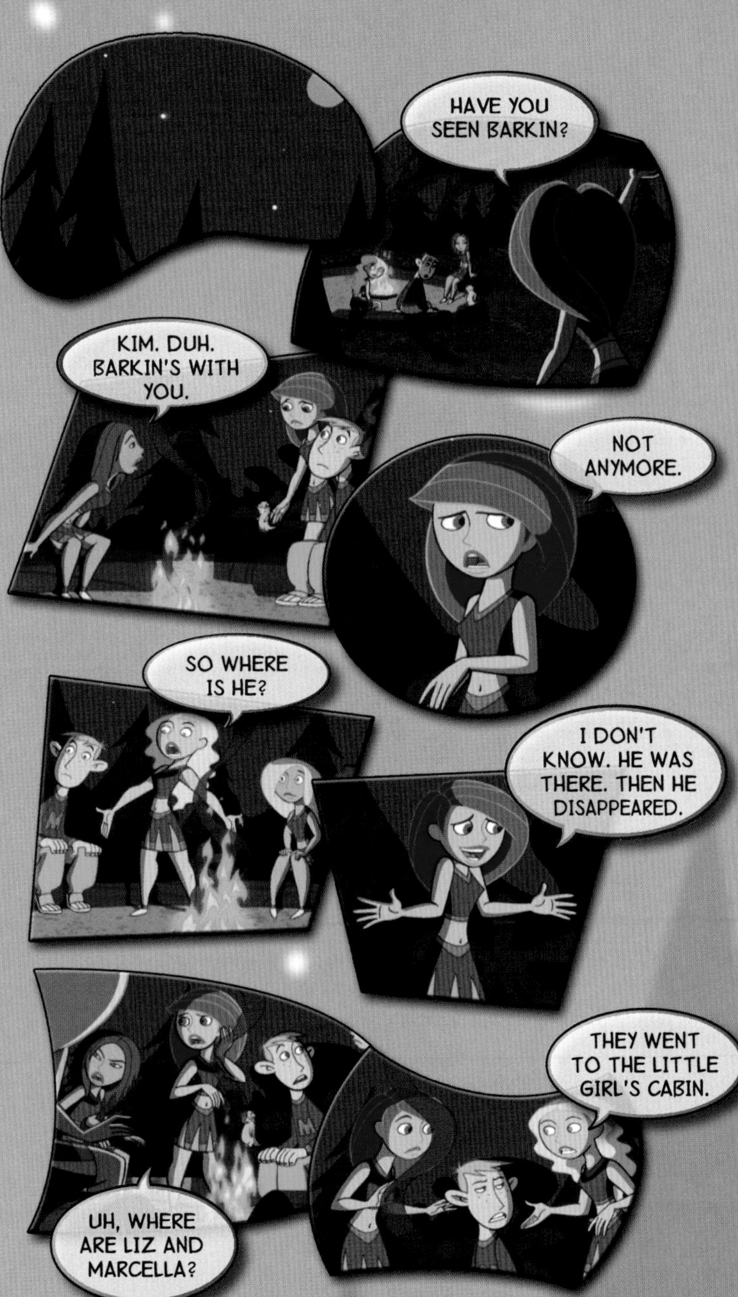
HAVE YOU SEEN BARKIN?
KIM. DUH. BARKIN'S WITH YOU.
NOT ANYMORE.
SO WHERE IS HE?
I DON'T KNOW. HE WAS THERE. THEN HE DISAPPEARED.
UH, WHERE ARE LIZ AND MARCELLA?
THEY WENT TO THE LITTLE GIRL'S CABIN.

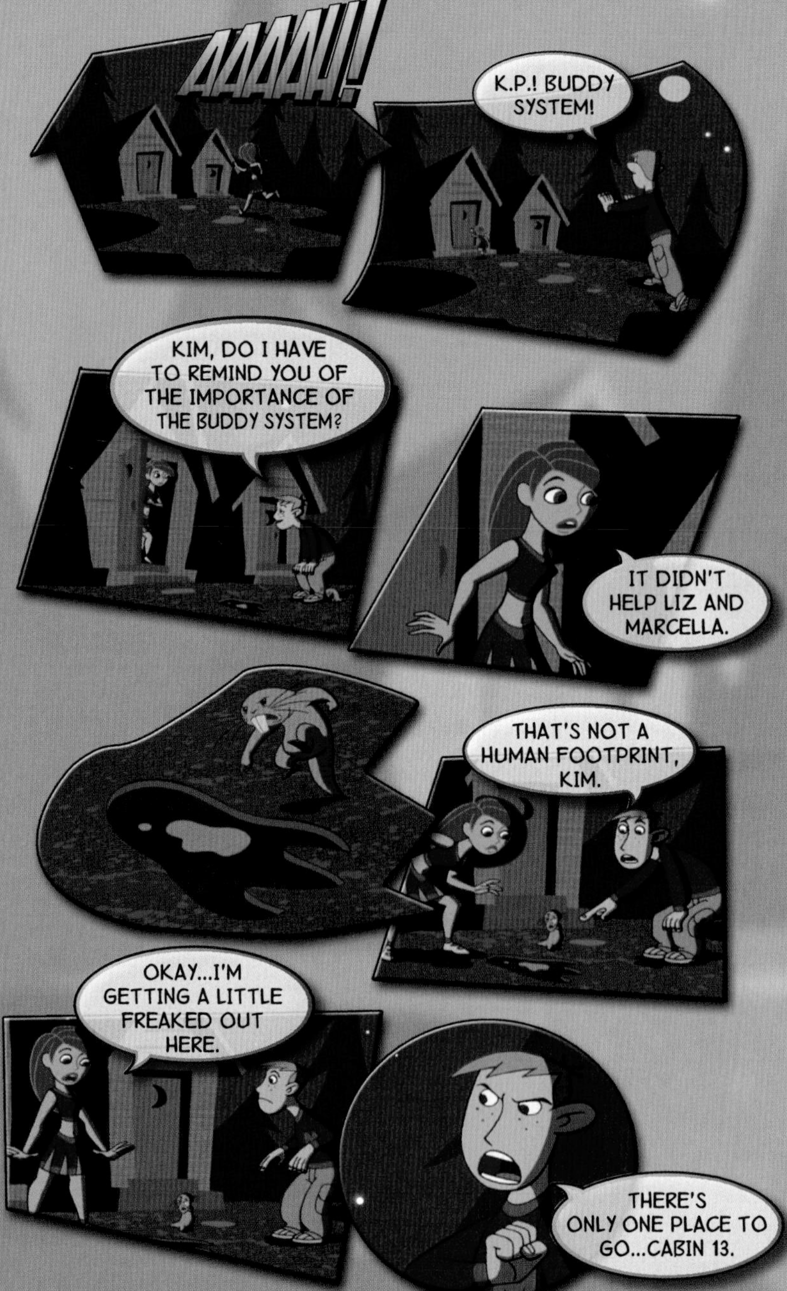
AAAAH!
K.P.! BUDDY SYSTEM!
KIM, DO I HAVE TO REMIND YOU OF THE IMPORTANCE OF THE BUDDY SYSTEM?
IT DIDN'T HELP LIZ AND MARCELLA.
THAT'S NOT A HUMAN FOOTPRINT, KIM.
OKAY...I'M GETTING A LITTLE FREAKED OUT HERE.
THERE'S ONLY ONE PLACE TO GO...CABIN 13.

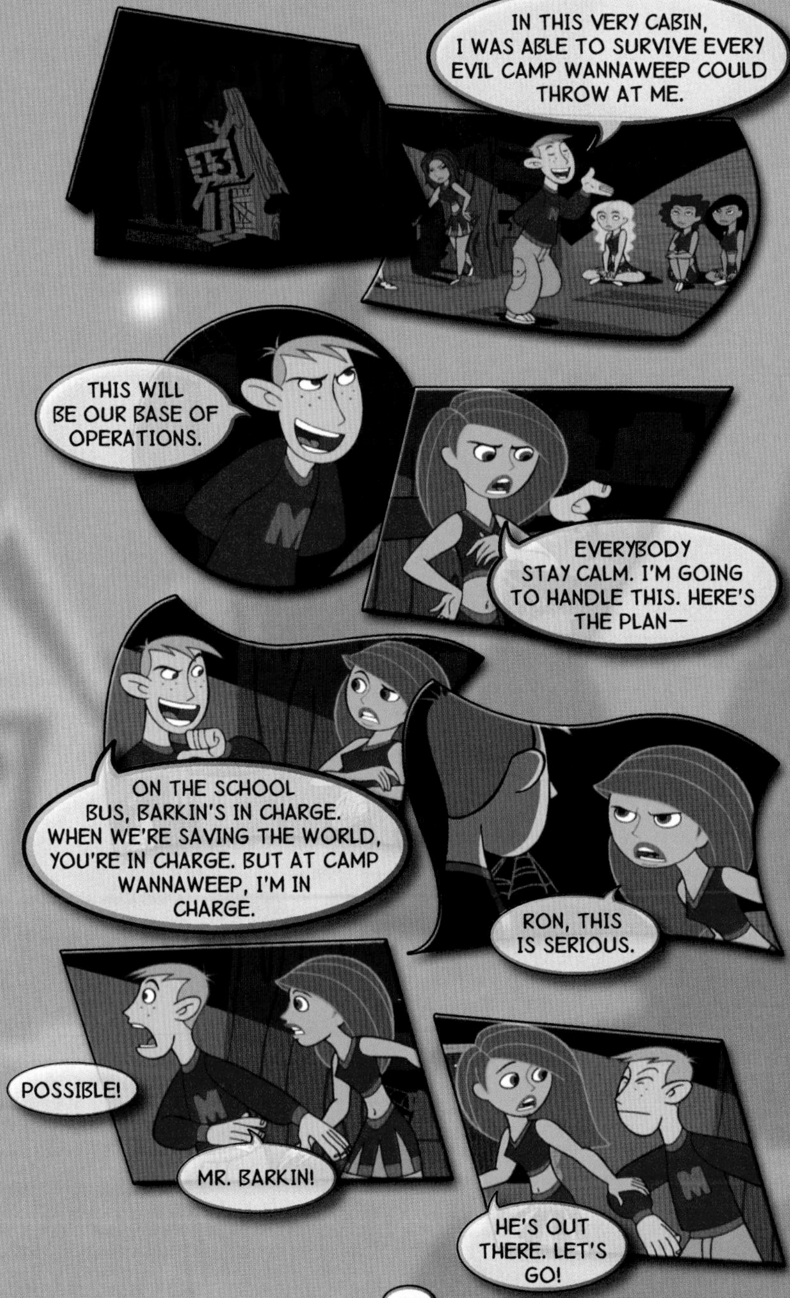
IN THIS VERY CABIN, I WAS ABLE TO SURVIVE EVERY EVIL CAMP WANNAWEEP COULD THROW AT ME.
THIS WILL BE OUR BASE OF OPERATIONS.
EVERYBODY STAY CALM. I'M GOING TO HANDLE THIS. HERE'S THE PLAN—
ON THE SCHOOL BUS, BARKIN'S IN CHARGE. WHEN WE'RE SAVING THE WORLD, YOU'RE IN CHARGE. BUT AT CAMP WANNAWEEP, I'M IN CHARGE.
RON, THIS IS SERIOUS.
POSSIBLE!
MR. BARKIN!
HE'S OUT THERE. LET'S GO!

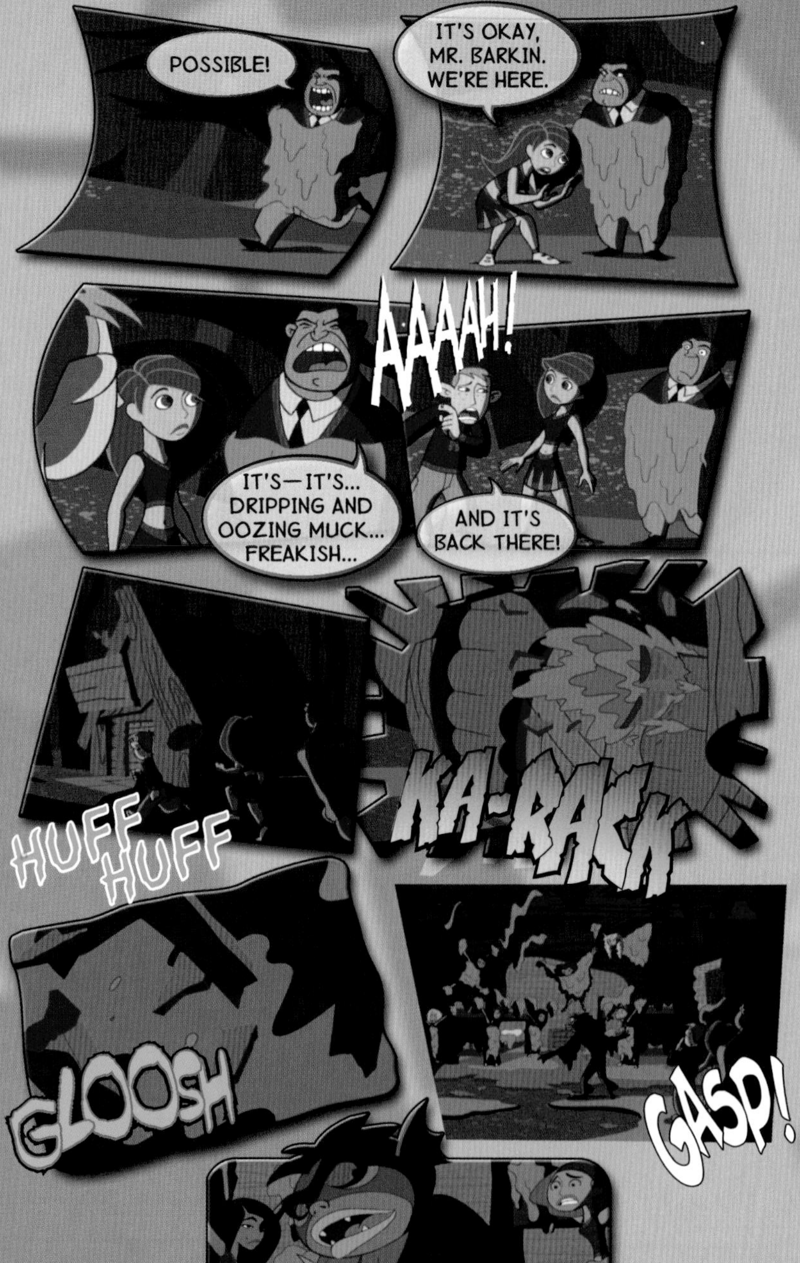
POSSIBLE!
IT'S OKAY, MR. BARKIN. WE'RE HERE.
AAAAH!
IT'S—IT'S... DRIPPING AND OOZING MUCK... FREAKISH...
AND IT'S BACK THERE!
HUFF HUFF
KA-RACK
GLOOSH
GASP!

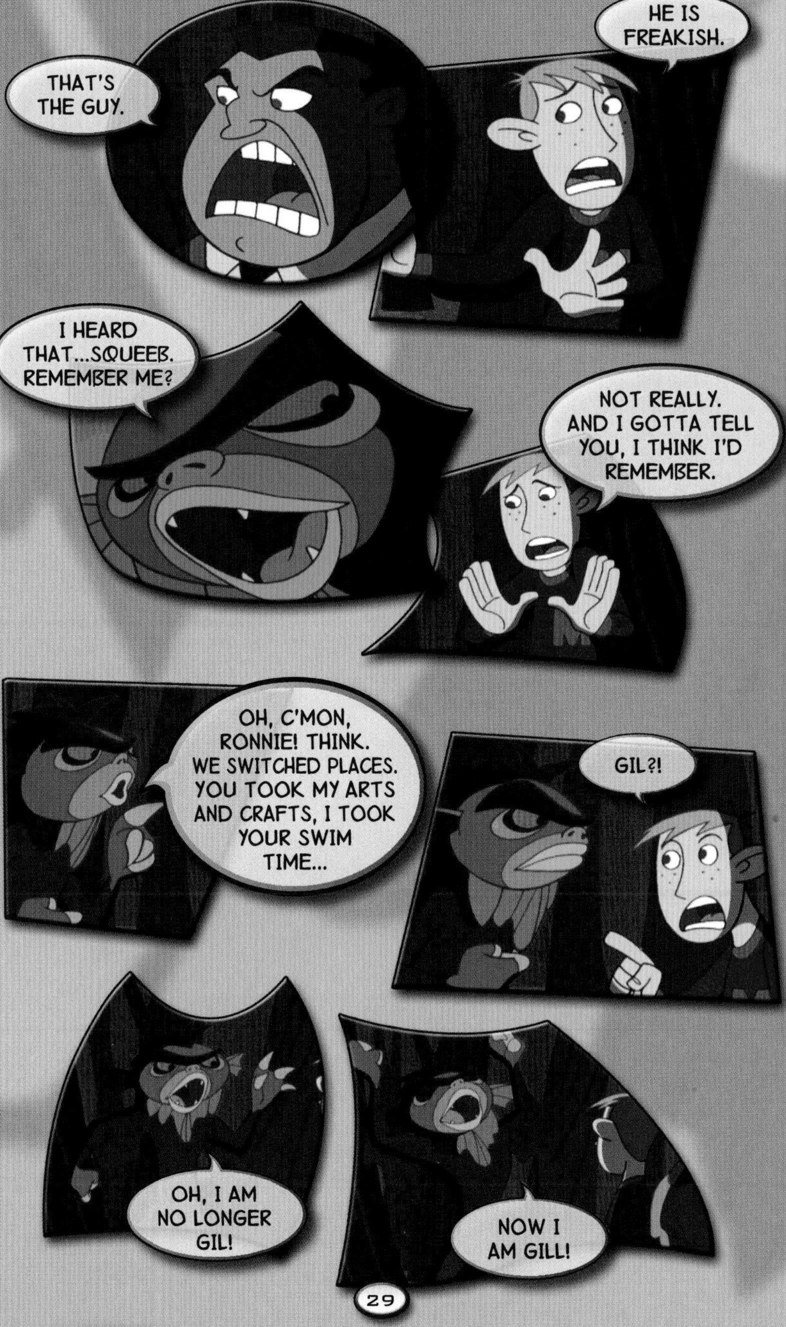
THAT'S THE GUY.
HE IS FREAKISH.
I HEARD THAT...SQUEEB. REMEMBER ME?
NOT REALLY. AND I GOTTA TELL YOU, I THINK I'D REMEMBER.
OH, C'MON, RONNIE! THINK. WE SWITCHED PLACES. YOU TOOK MY ARTS AND CRAFTS, I TOOK YOUR SWIM TIME...
GIL?!
OH, I AM NO LONGER GIL!
NOW I AM GILL!

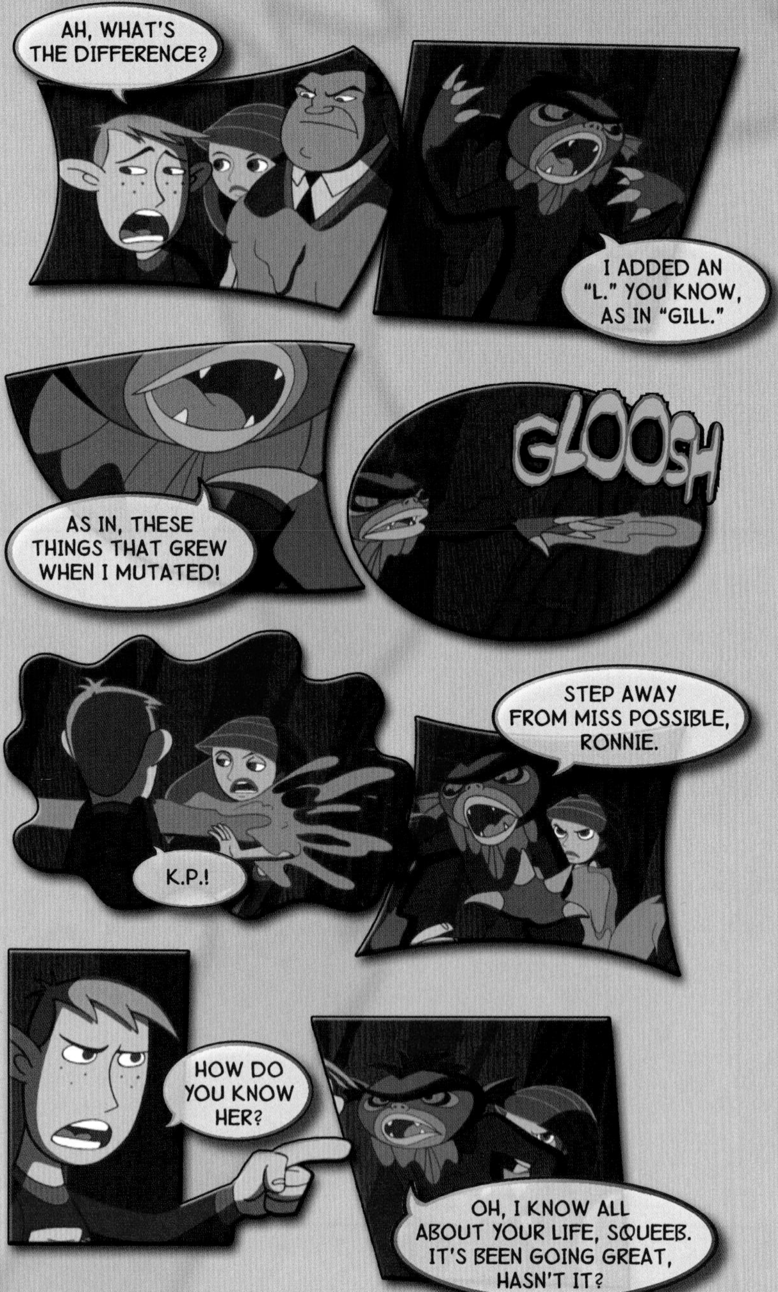
AH, WHAT'S THE DIFFERENCE?
I ADDED AN "L." YOU KNOW, AS IN "GILL."
AS IN, THESE THINGS THAT GREW WHEN I MUTATED!
GLOOSH
K.P.!
STEP AWAY FROM MISS POSSIBLE, RONNIE.
HOW DO YOU KNOW HER?
OH, I KNOW ALL ABOUT YOUR LIFE, SQUEEB. IT'S BEEN GOING GREAT, HASN'T IT?

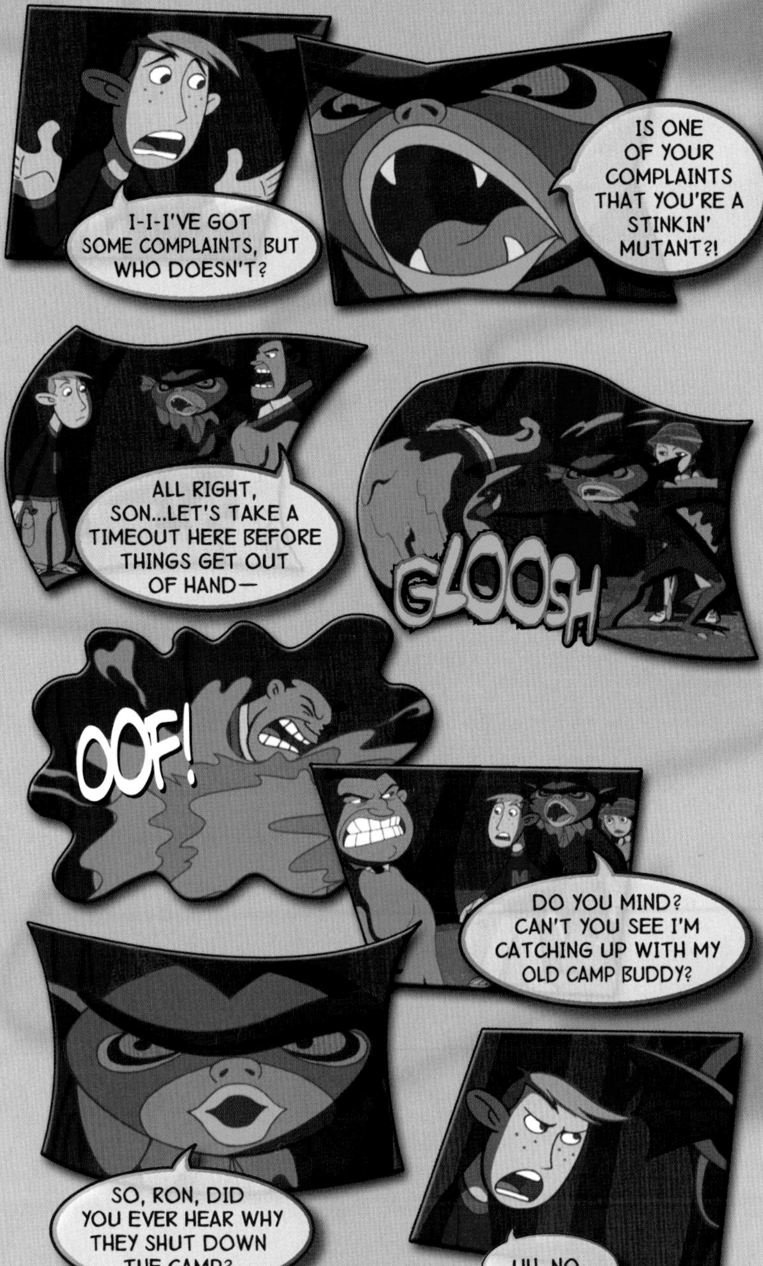
I-I-I'VE GOT SOME COMPLAINTS, BUT WHO DOESN'T?
IS ONE OF YOUR COMPLAINTS THAT YOU'RE A STINKIN' MUTANT?!
ALL RIGHT, SON...LET'S TAKE A TIMEOUT HERE BEFORE THINGS GET OUT OF HAND—
GLOOSH
OOF!
DO YOU MIND? CAN'T YOU SEE I'M CATCHING UP WITH MY OLD CAMP BUDDY?
SO, RON, DID YOU EVER HEAR WHY THEY SHUT DOWN THE CAMP?
UH, NO.

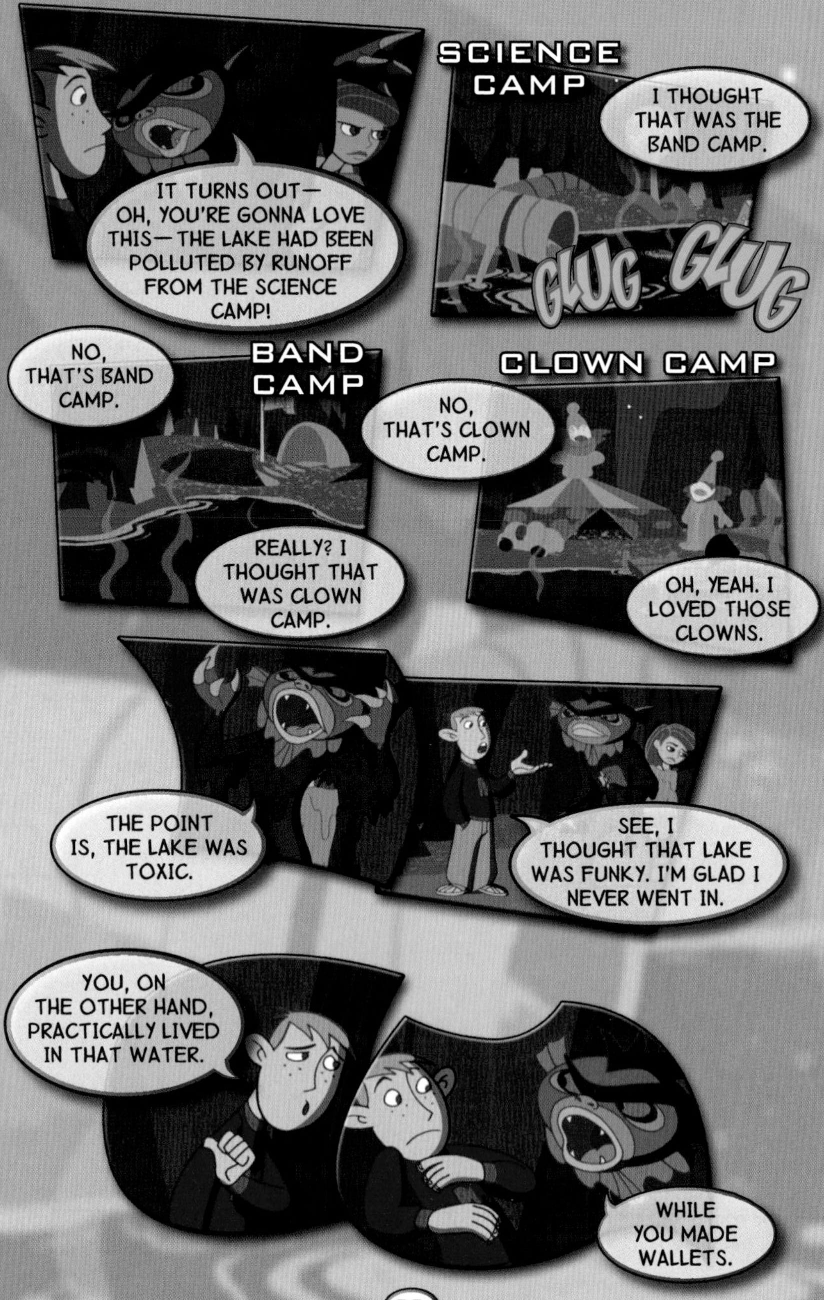
IT TURNS OUT— OH, YOU'RE GONNA LOVE THIS— THE LAKE HAD BEEN POLLUTED BY RUNOFF FROM THE SCIENCE CAMP!
SCIENCE CAMP
I THOUGHT THAT WAS THE BAND CAMP.
GLUG GLUG
NO, THAT'S BAND CAMP.
BAND CAMP
REALLY? I THOUGHT THAT WAS CLOWN CAMP.
CLOWN CAMP
NO, THAT'S CLOWN CAMP.
OH, YEAH. I LOVED THOSE CLOWNS.
THE POINT IS, THE LAKE WAS TOXIC.
SEE, I THOUGHT THAT LAKE WAS FUNKY. I'M GLAD I NEVER WENT IN.
YOU, ON THE OTHER HAND, PRACTICALLY LIVED IN THAT WATER.
WHILE YOU MADE WALLETS.

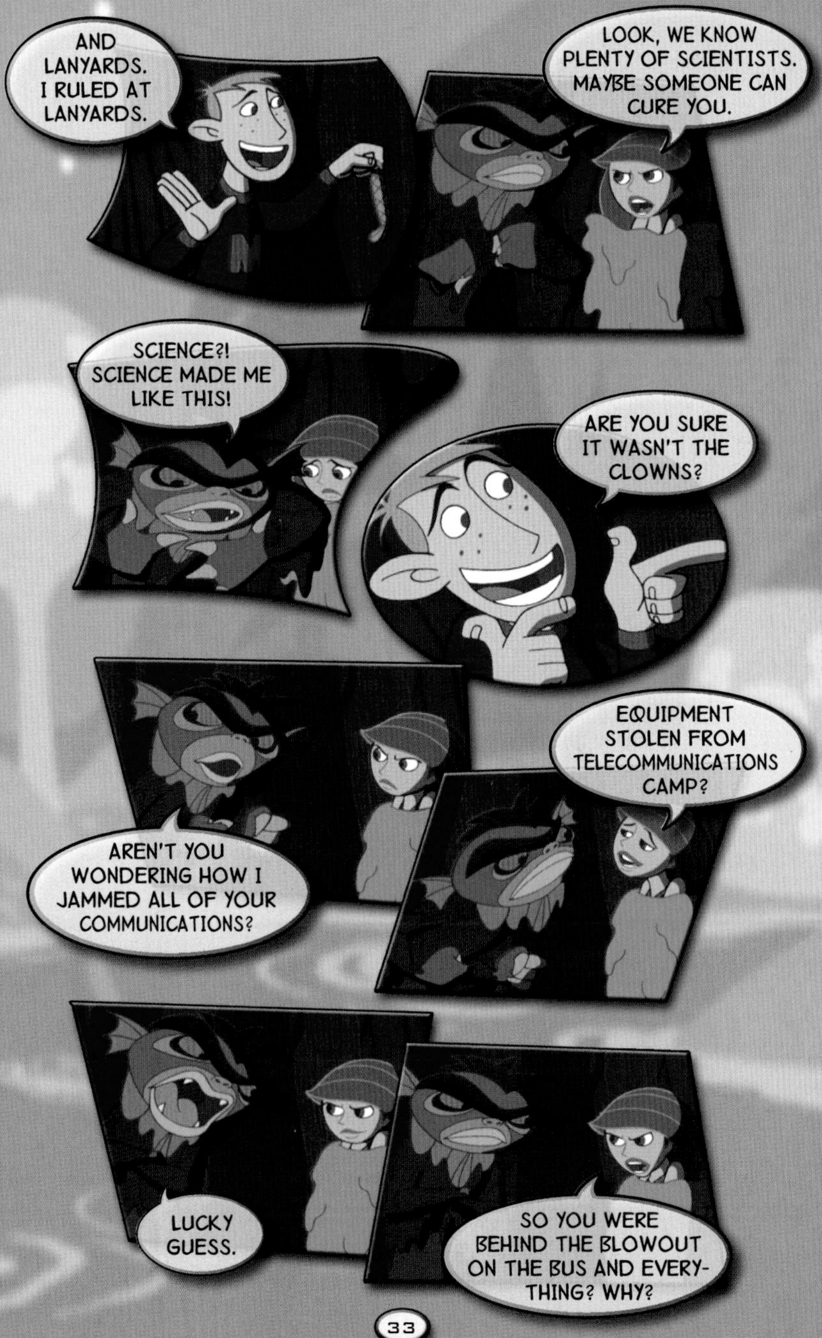
AND LANYARDS. I RULED AT LANYARDS.
LOOK, WE KNOW PLENTY OF SCIENTISTS. MAYBE SOMEONE CAN CURE YOU.
SCIENCE?! SCIENCE MADE ME LIKE THIS!
ARE YOU SURE IT WASN'T THE CLOWNS?
AREN'T YOU WONDERING HOW I JAMMED ALL OF YOUR COMMUNICATIONS?
EQUIPMENT STOLEN FROM TELECOMMUNICATIONS CAMP?
LUCKY GUESS.
SO YOU WERE BEHIND THE BLOWOUT ON THE BUS AND EVERY-THING? WHY?

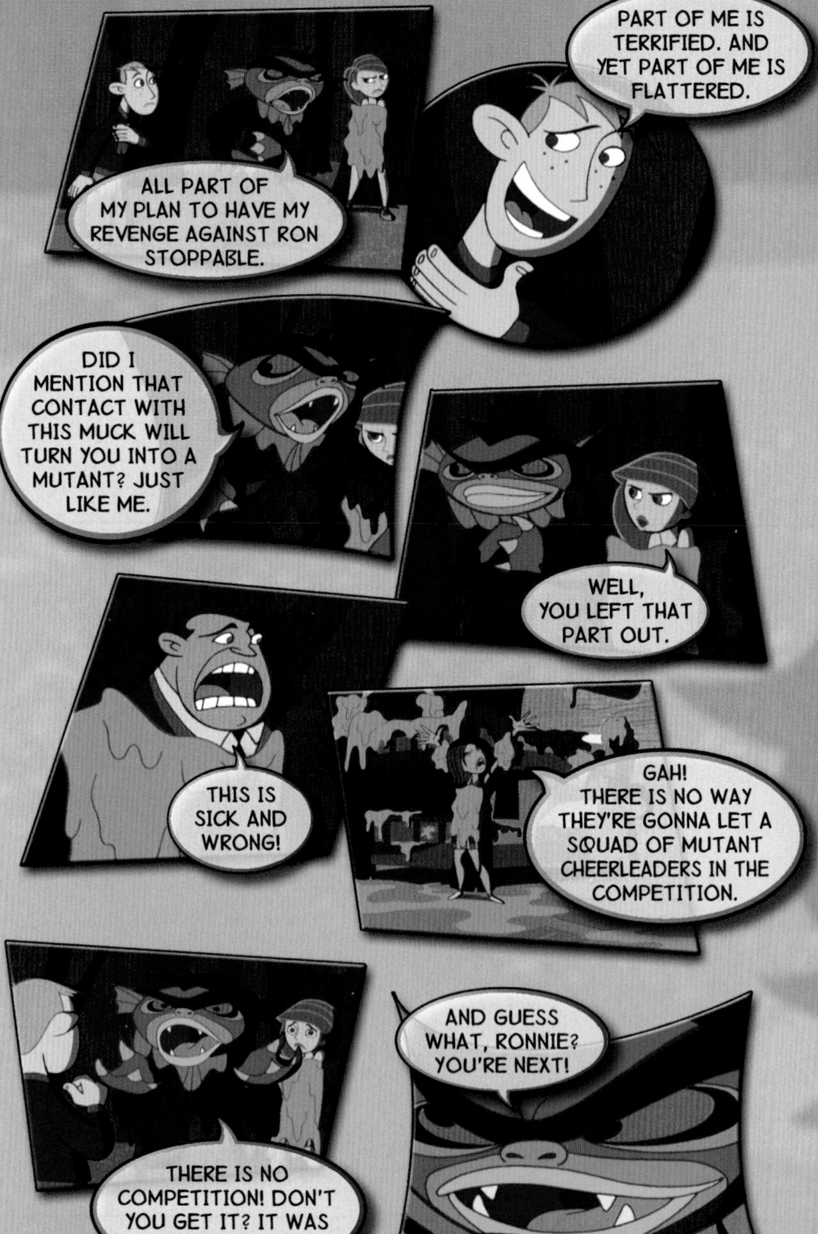
ALL PART OF MY PLAN TO HAVE MY REVENGE AGAINST RON STOPPABLE.
PART OF ME IS TERRIFIED. AND YET PART OF ME IS FLATTERED.
DID I MENTION THAT CONTACT WITH THIS MUCK WILL TURN YOU INTO A MUTANT? JUST LIKE ME.
WELL, YOU LEFT THAT PART OUT.
THIS IS SICK AND WRONG!
GAH! THERE IS NO WAY THEY'RE GONNA LET A SQUAD OF MUTANT CHEERLEADERS IN THE COMPETITION.
THERE IS NO COMPETITION! DON'T YOU GET IT? IT WAS ALL A TRAP!
AND GUESS WHAT, RONNIE? YOU'RE NEXT!

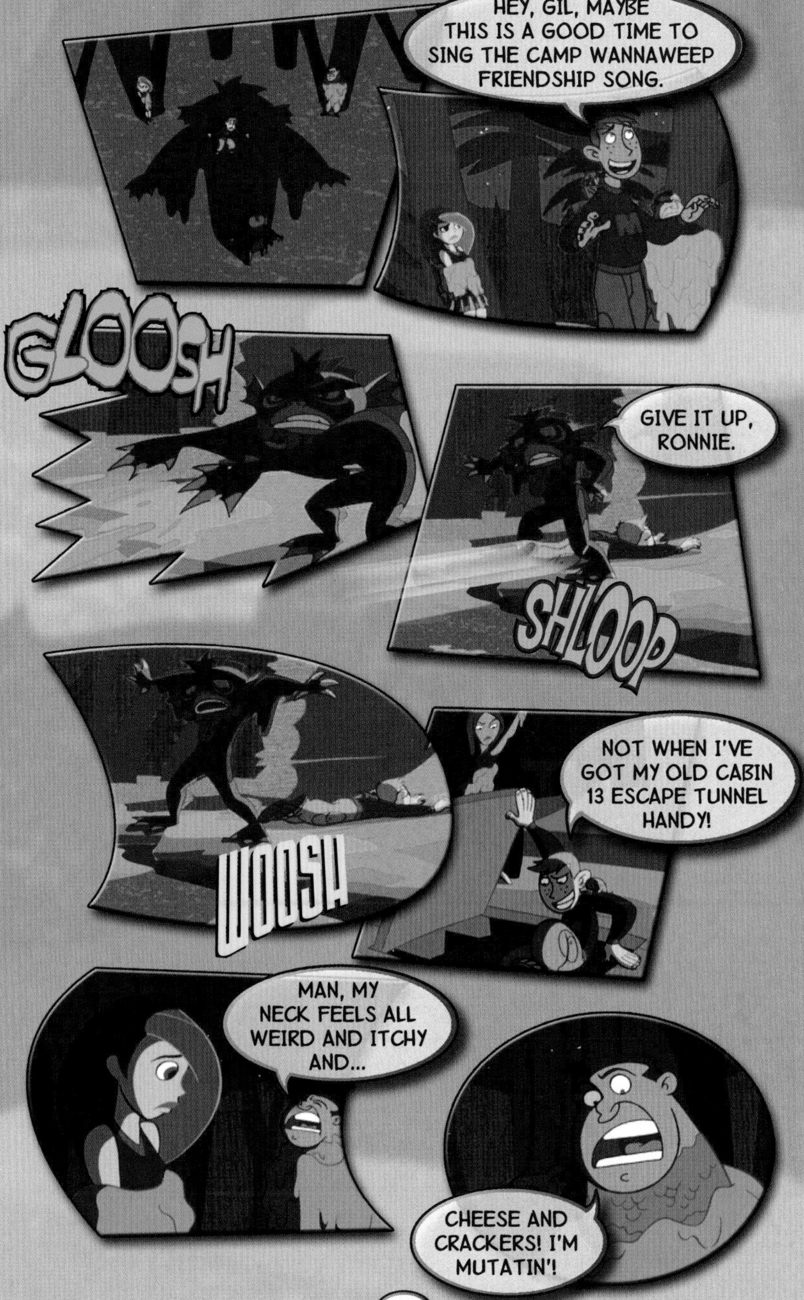
HEY, GIL, MAYBE THIS IS A GOOD TIME TO SING THE CAMP WANNAWEEP FRIENDSHIP SONG.
GLOOSH
GIVE IT UP, RONNIE.
SHLOOP
WOOSH
NOT WHEN I'VE GOT MY OLD CABIN 13 ESCAPE TUNNEL HANDY!
MAN, MY NECK FEELS ALL WEIRD AND ITCHY AND...
CHEESE AND CRACKERS! I'M MUTATIN'!

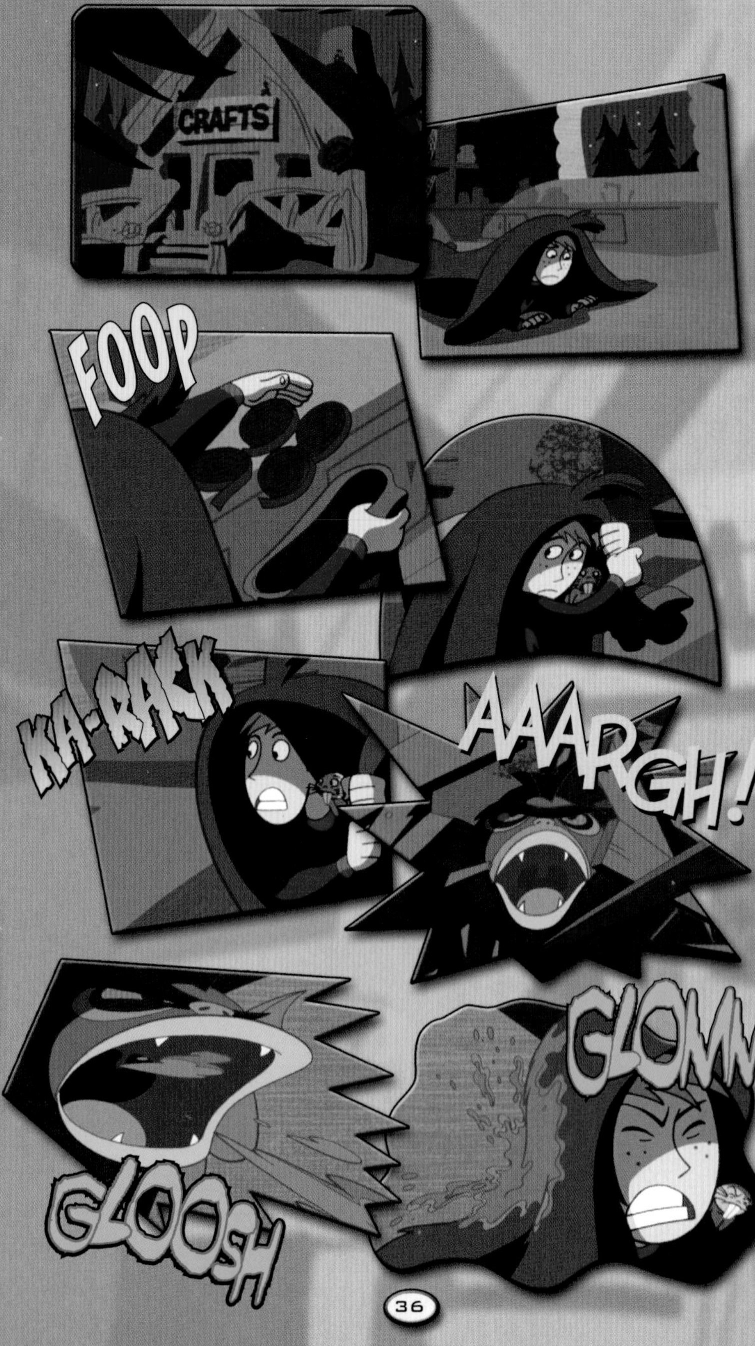
CRAFTS
FOOP
KA-RACK
AAARGH!
GLOMMF
GLOOSH

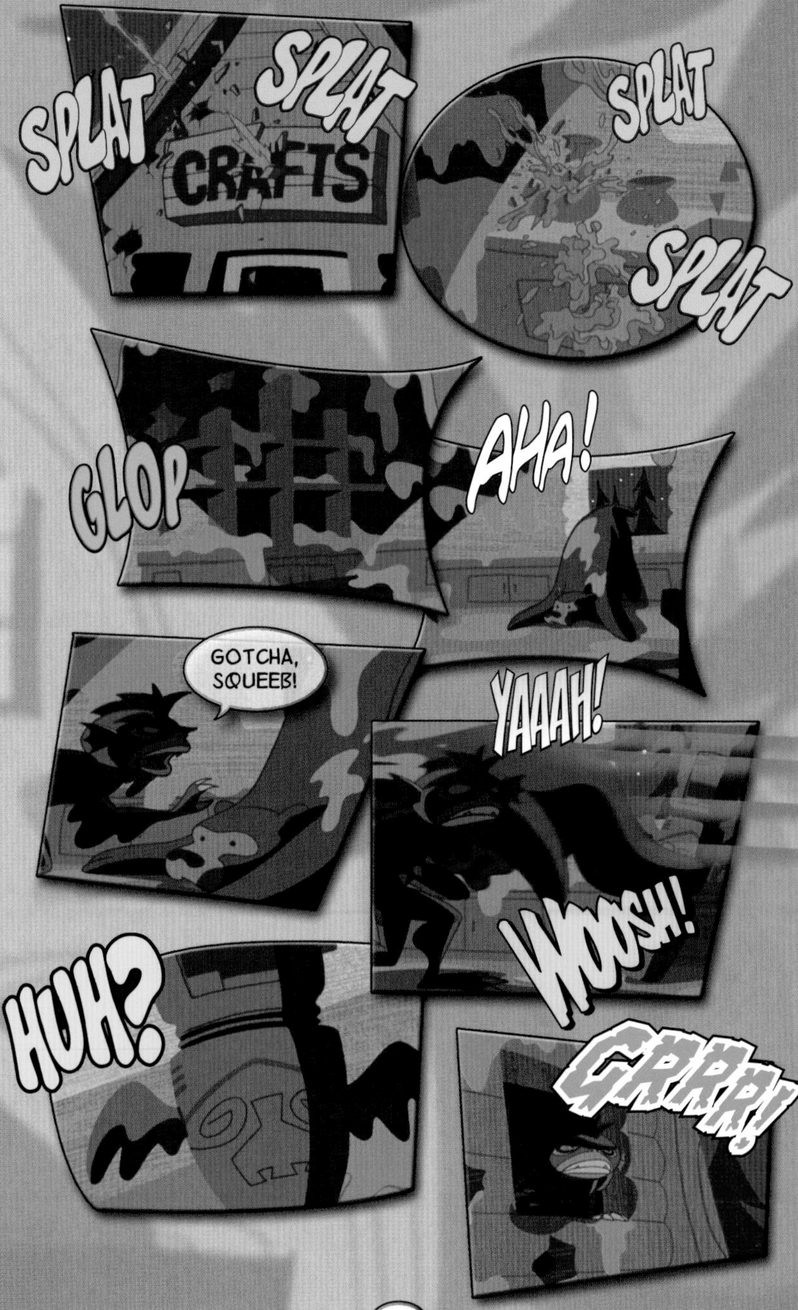
SPLAT
SPLAT
CRAFTS
SPLAT
SPLAT
GLOP
AHA!
GOTCHA, SQUEEB!
YAAAH!
WOOSH!
HUH?
GRRR!

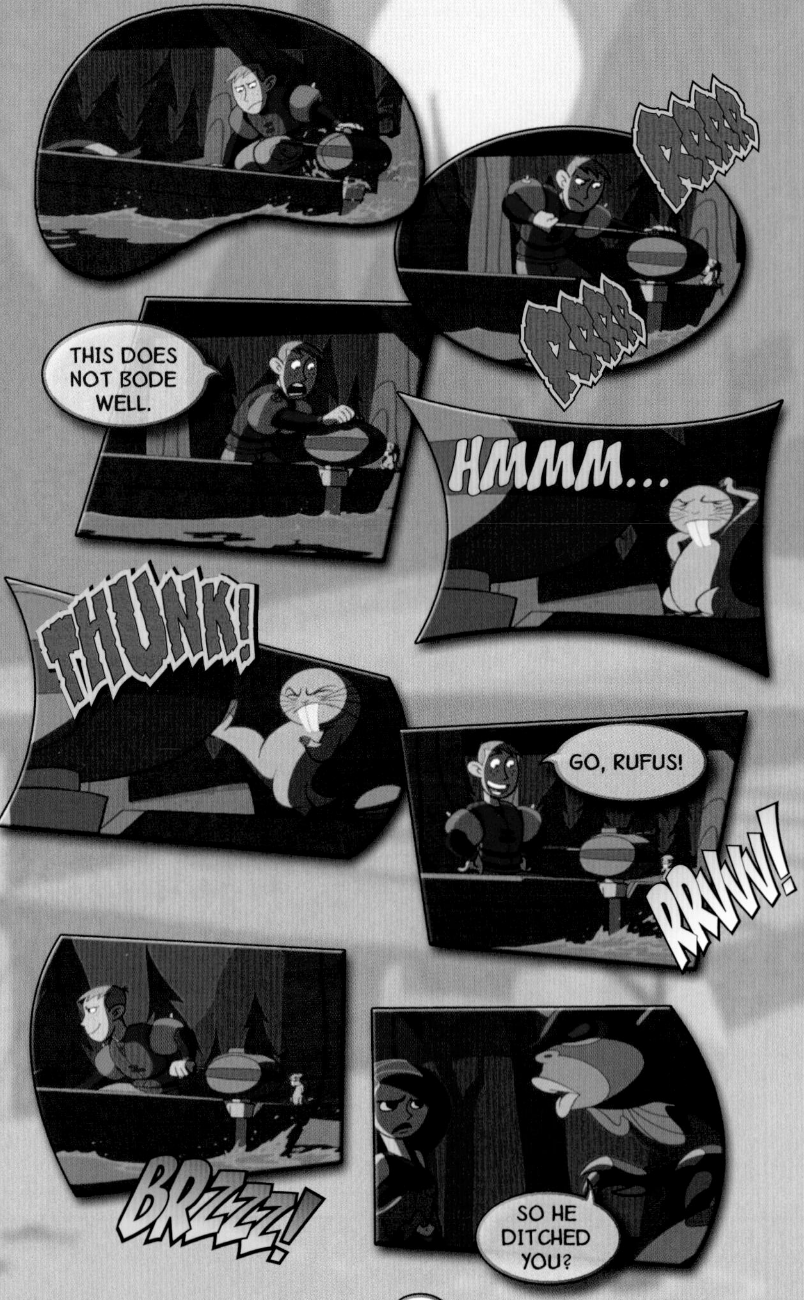
THIS DOES NOT BODE WELL.
HMMM...
THUNK!
GO, RUFUS!
SO HE DITCHED YOU?

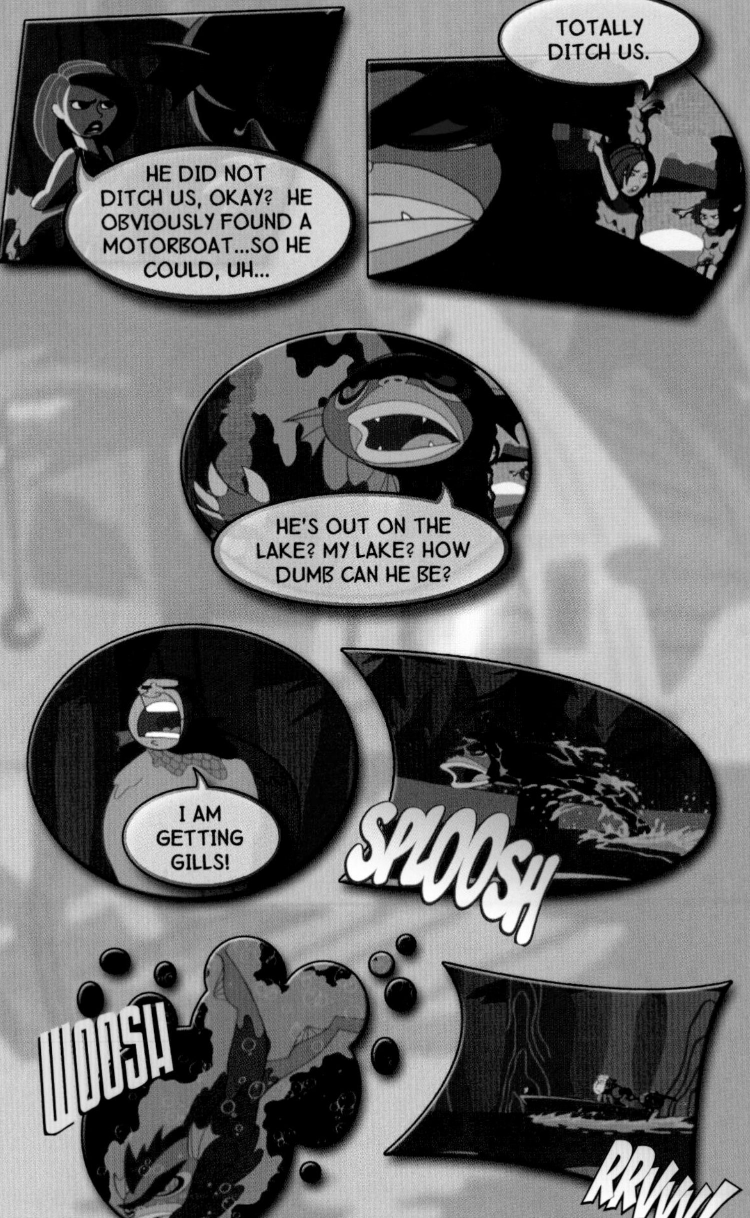
HE DID NOT DITCH US, OKAY? HE OBVIOUSLY FOUND A MOTORBOAT...SO HE COULD, UH...
TOTALLY DITCH US.
HE'S OUT ON THE LAKE? MY LAKE? HOW DUMB CAN HE BE?
I AM GETTING GILLS!
SPLOOSH
WOOSH
RRVVV!

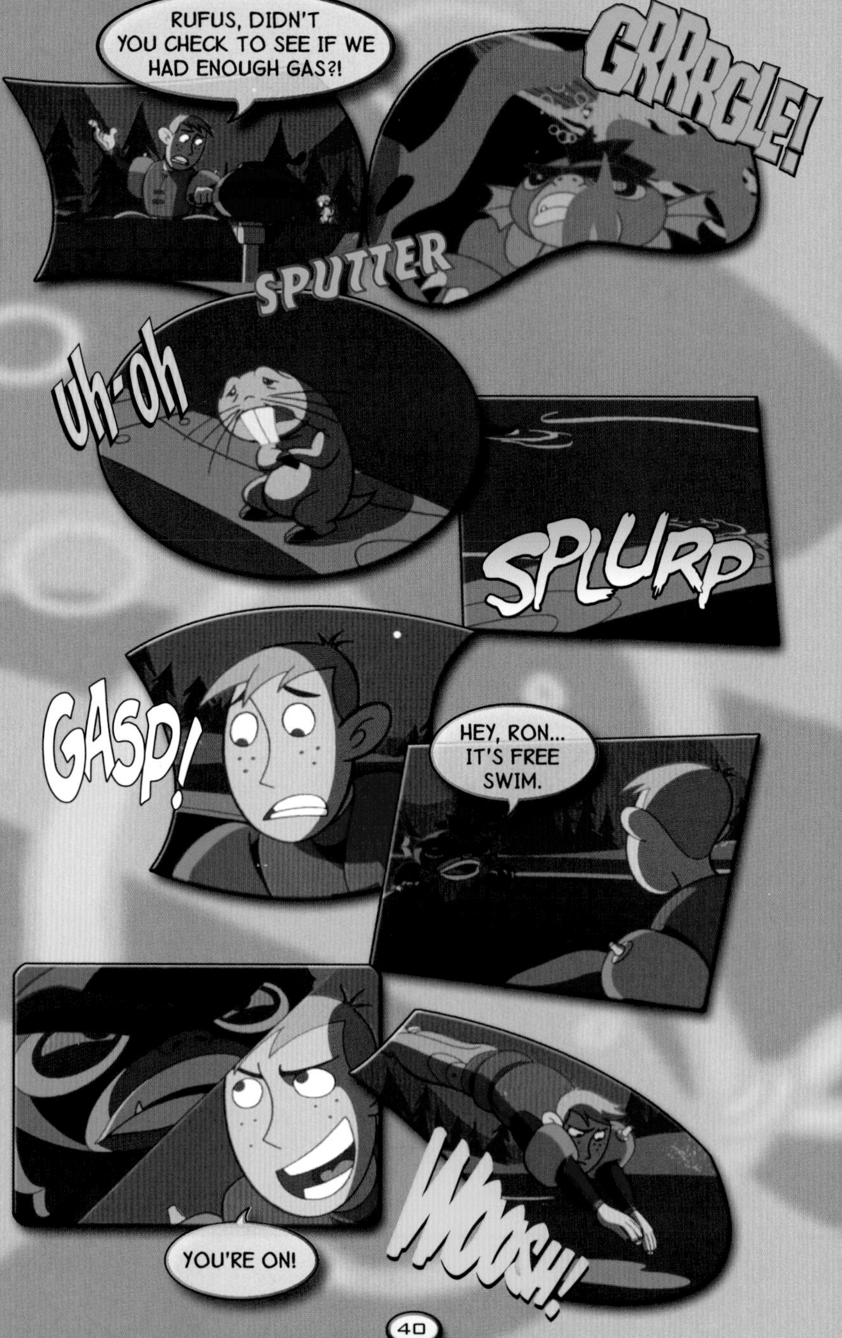

RUFUS, DIDN'T YOU CHECK TO SEE IF WE HAD ENOUGH GAS?!
GRRRGLE!
SPUTTER
uh-oh
SPLURP
GASP!
HEY, RON... IT'S FREE SWIM.
YOU'RE ON!
WOOSH!

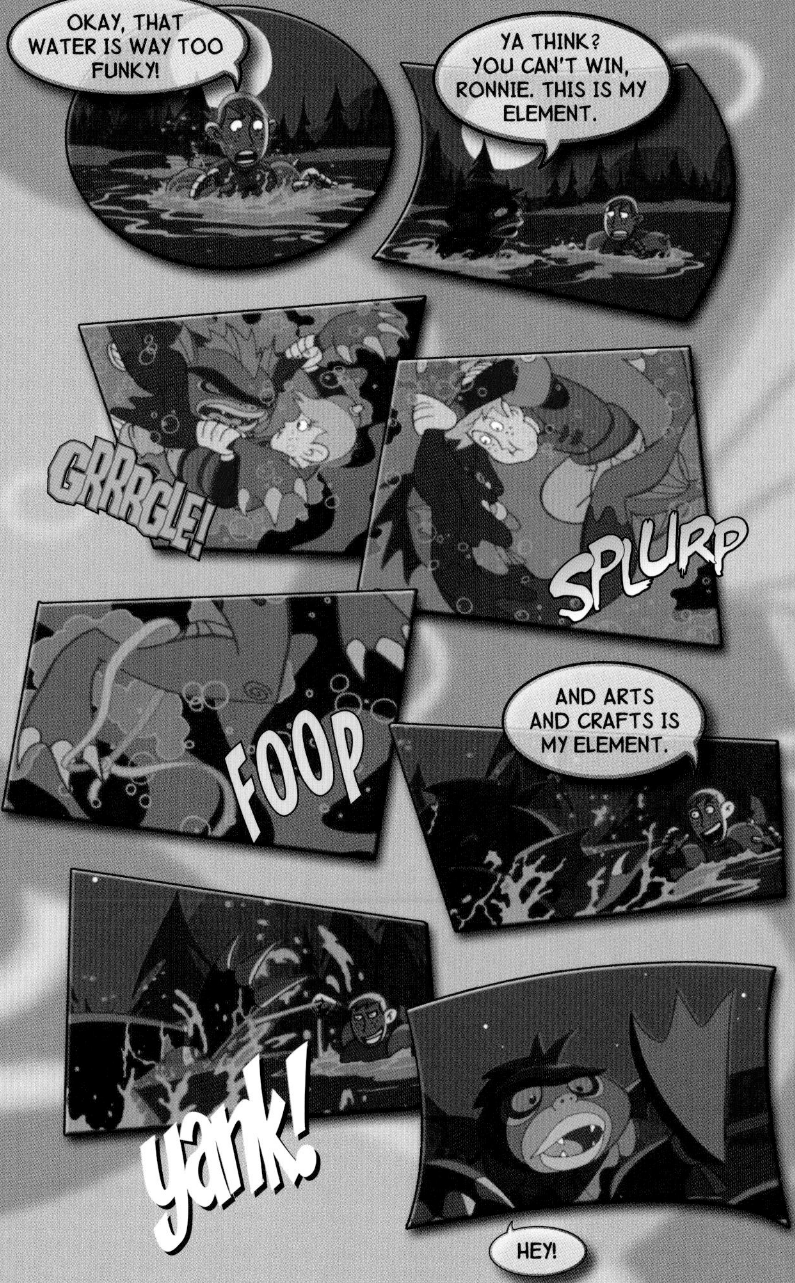
OKAY, THAT WATER IS WAY TOO FUNKY!
YA THINK? YOU CAN'T WIN, RONNIE. THIS IS MY ELEMENT.
GRRRGLE!
SPLURP
FOOP
AND ARTS AND CRAFTS IS MY ELEMENT.
yank!
HEY!

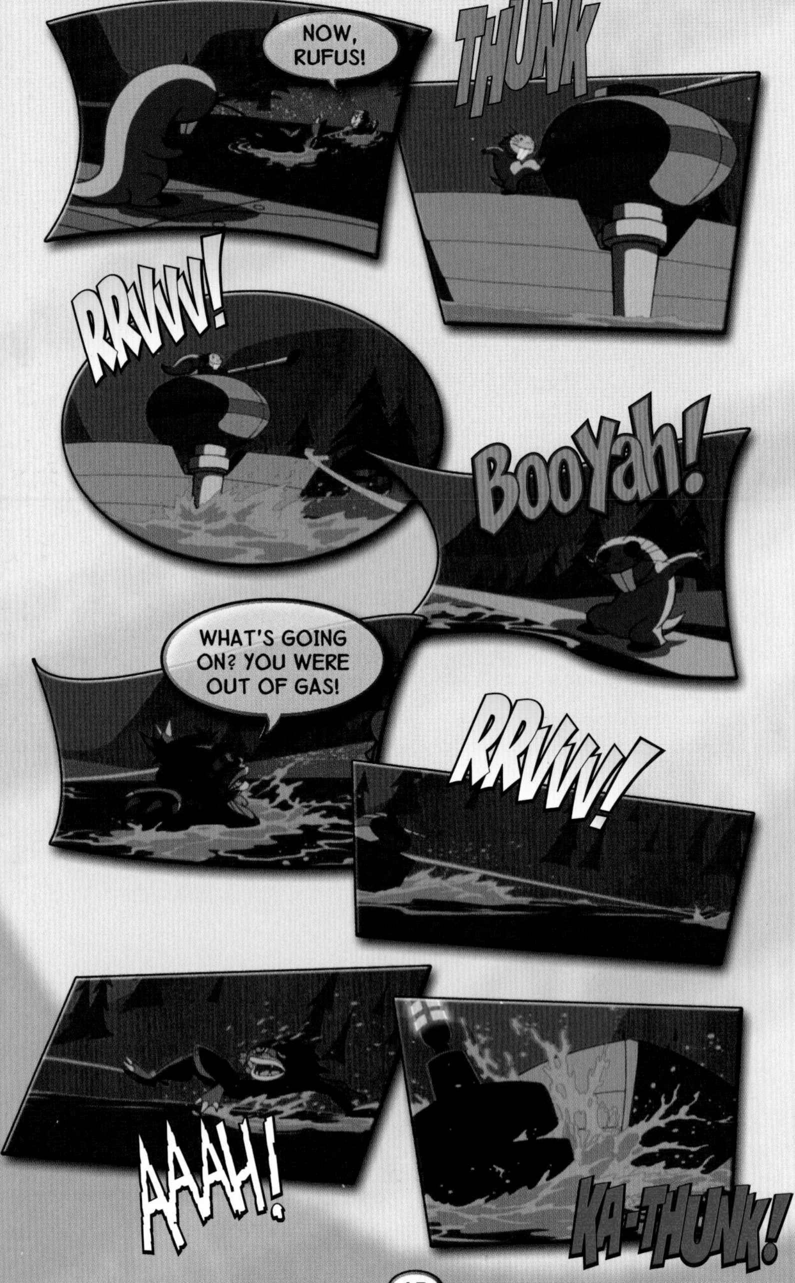
NOW, RUFUS!
THUNK
RRVVV!
BOOYAH!
WHAT'S GOING ON? YOU WERE OUT OF GAS!
RRVVV!
AAAH!
KA-THUNK!

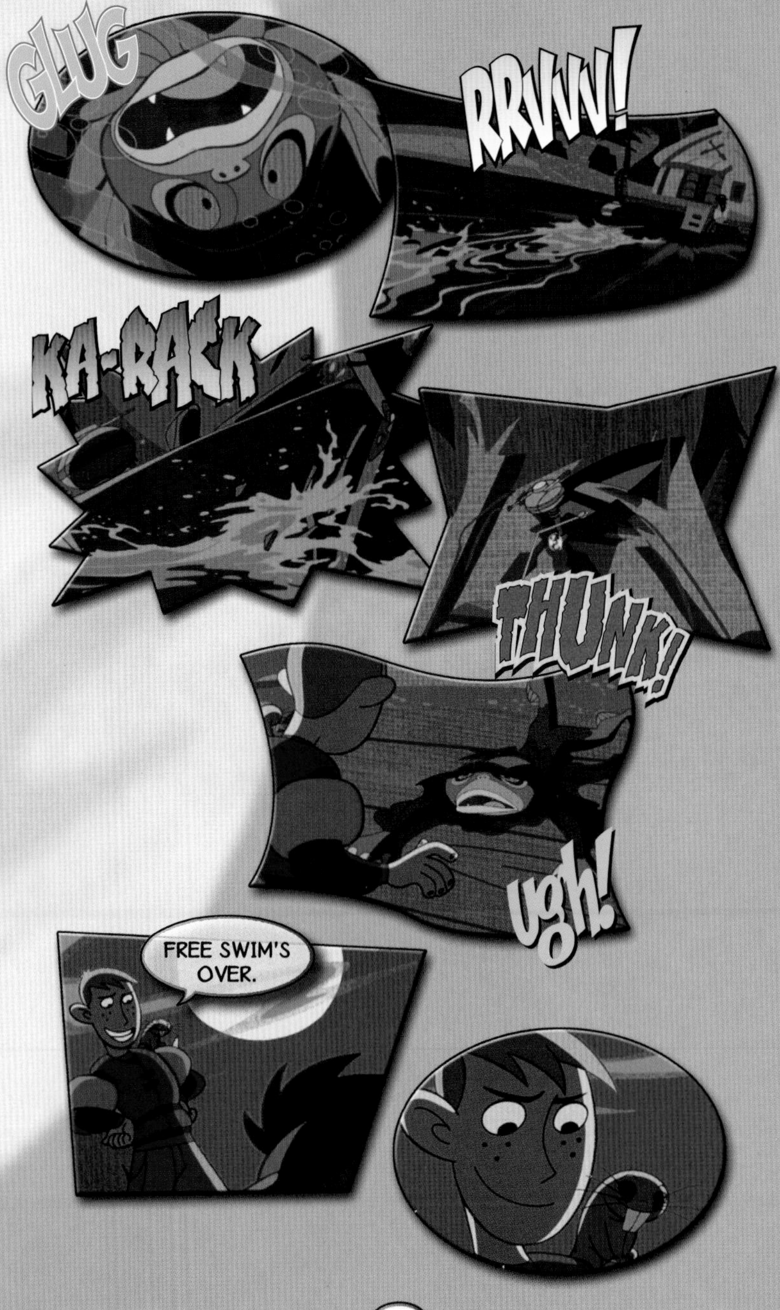
GLUG
RRVVV!
KA-RACK
THUNK!
UGH!
FREE SWIM'S OVER.

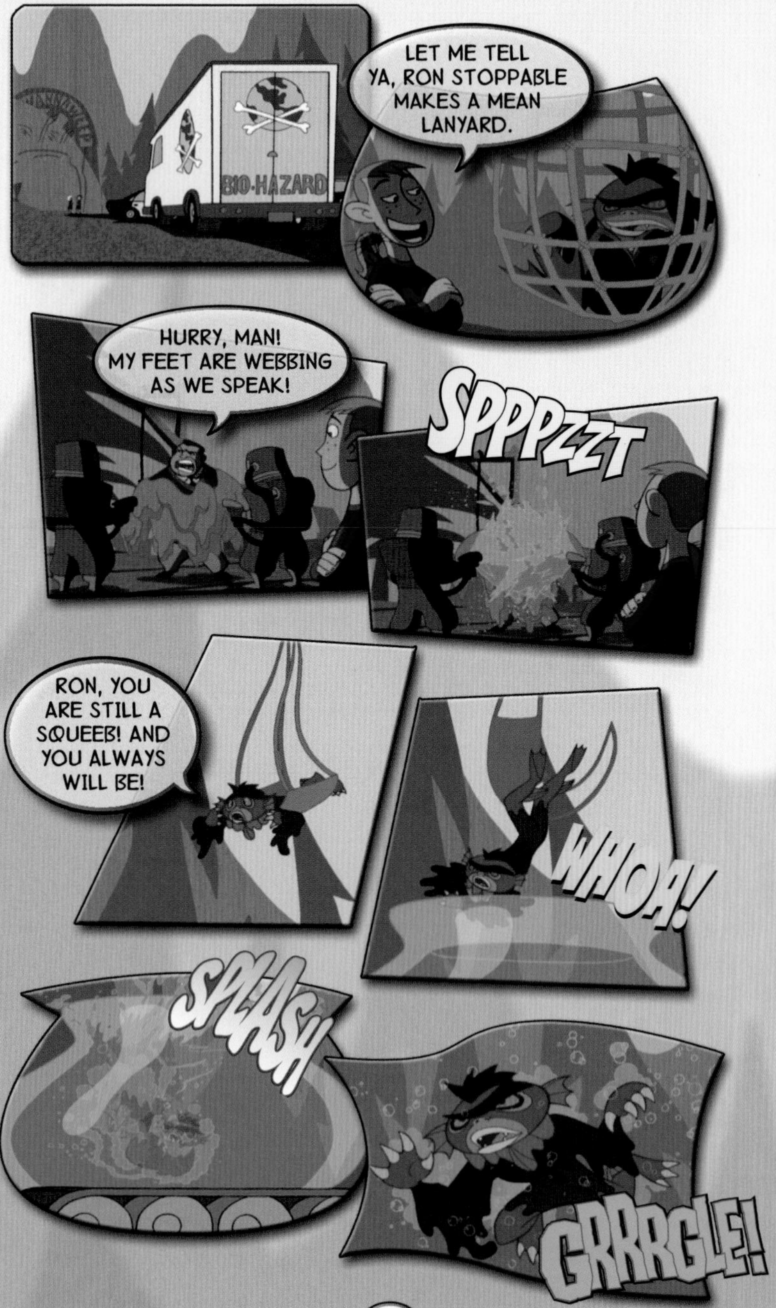
BIO-HAZARD
LET ME TELL YA, RON STOPPABLE MAKES A MEAN LANYARD.
HURRY, MAN! MY FEET ARE WEBBING AS WE SPEAK!
SPPPZZZT
RON, YOU ARE STILL A SQUEEB! AND YOU ALWAYS WILL BE!
WHOA!
SPLASH
GRRRGLE!

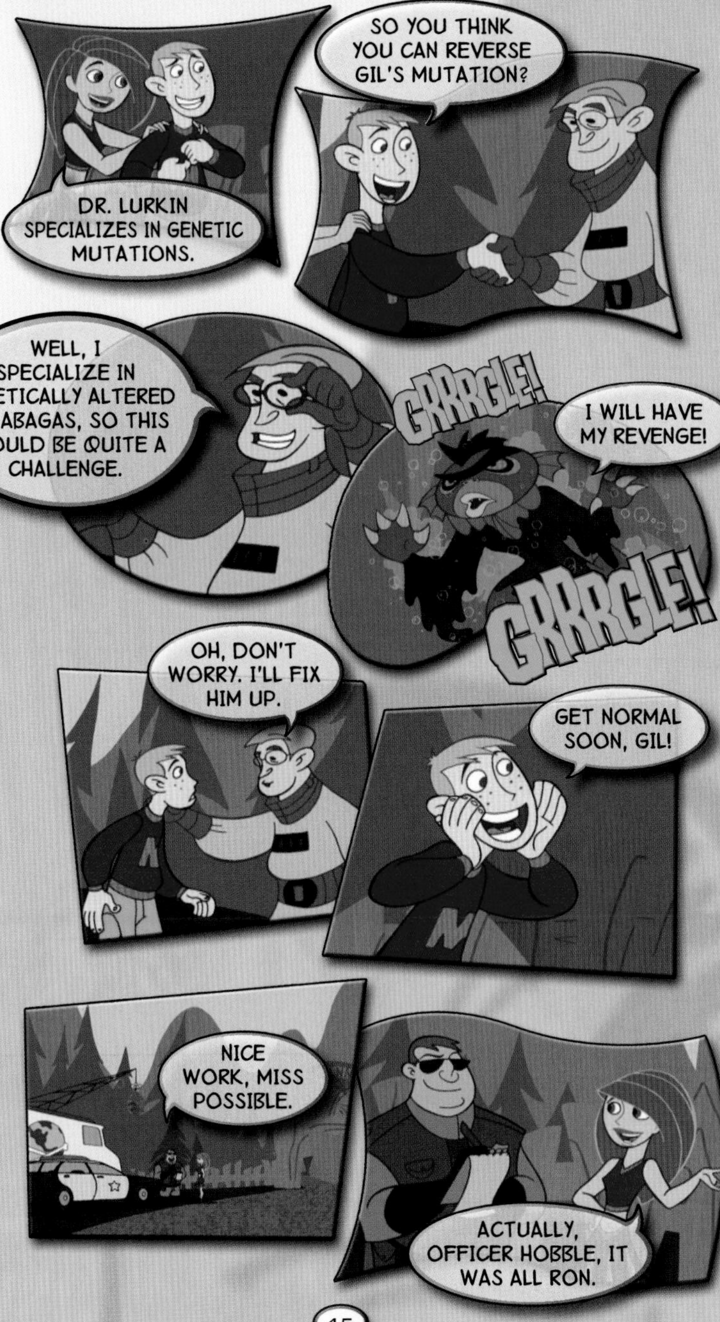
DR. LURKIN SPECIALIZES IN GENETIC MUTATIONS.
SO YOU THINK YOU CAN REVERSE GIL'S MUTATION?
WELL, I SPECIALIZE IN GENETICALLY ALTERED RUTABAGAS, SO THIS SHOULD BE QUITE A CHALLENGE.
GRRRGLE!
I WILL HAVE MY REVENGE!
GRRRGLE!
OH, DON'T WORRY. I'LL FIX HIM UP.
GET NORMAL SOON, GIL!
NICE WORK, MISS POSSIBLE.
ACTUALLY, OFFICER HOBBLE, IT WAS ALL RON.

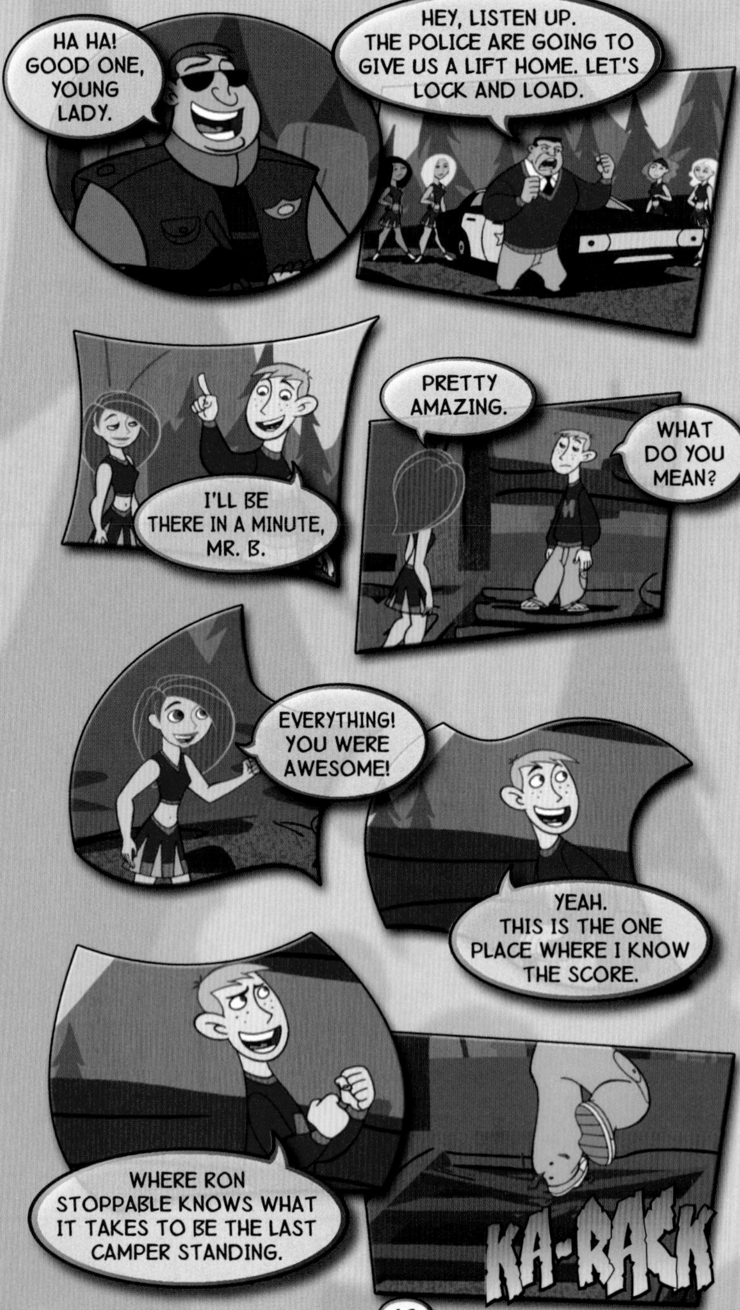
HA HA! GOOD ONE, YOUNG LADY.
HEY, LISTEN UP. THE POLICE ARE GOING TO GIVE US A LIFT HOME. LET'S LOCK AND LOAD.
I'LL BE THERE IN A MINUTE, MR. B.
PRETTY AMAZING.
WHAT DO YOU MEAN?
EVERYTHING! YOU WERE AWESOME!
YEAH. THIS IS THE ONE PLACE WHERE I KNOW THE SCORE.
WHERE RON STOPPABLE KNOWS WHAT IT TAKES TO BE THE LAST CAMPER STANDING.
KA-RACK

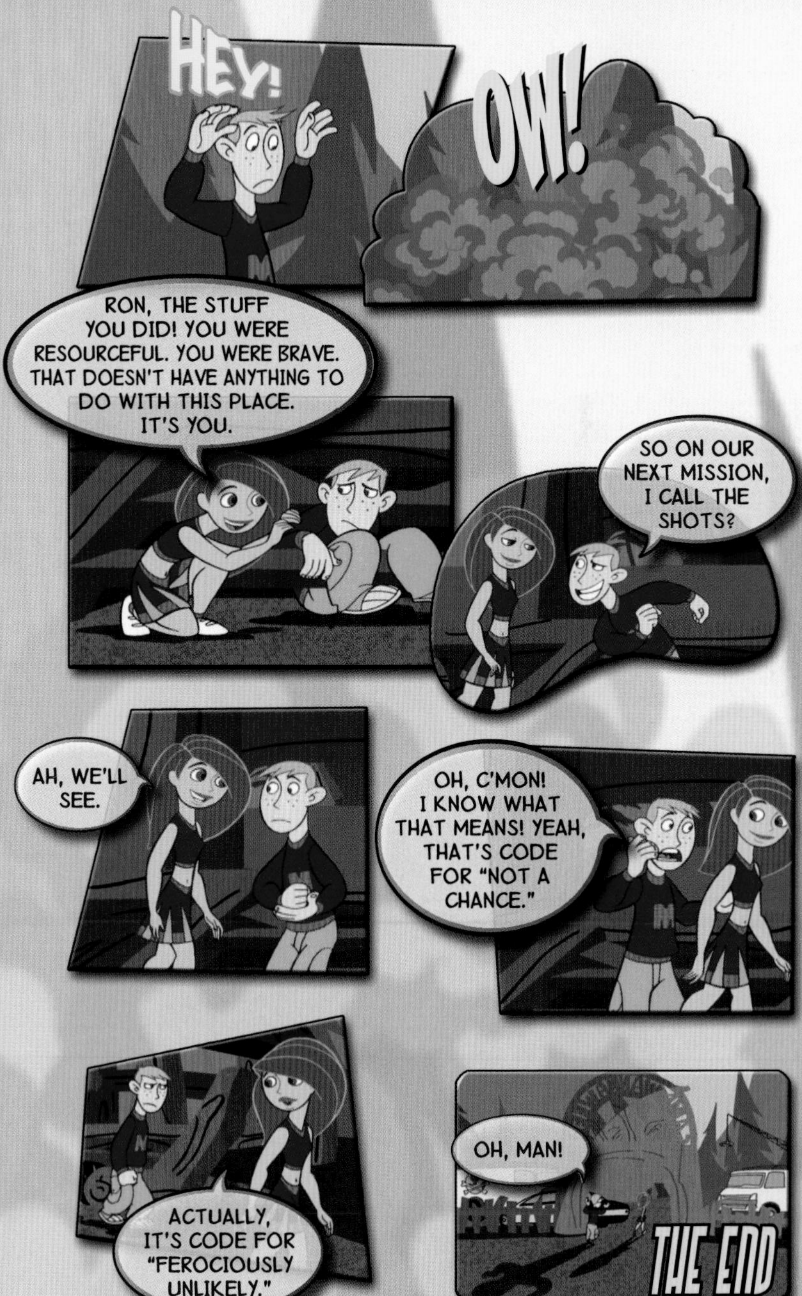
HEY!
OW!
RON, THE STUFF YOU DID! YOU WERE RESOURCEFUL. YOU WERE BRAVE. THAT DOESN'T HAVE ANYTHING TO DO WITH THIS PLACE. IT'S YOU.
SO ON OUR NEXT MISSION, I CALL THE SHOTS?
AH, WE'LL SEE.
OH, C'MON! I KNOW WHAT THAT MEANS! YEAH, THAT'S CODE FOR "NOT A CHANCE."
ACTUALLY, IT'S CODE FOR "FEROCIOUSLY UNLIKELY."
OH, MAN!
THE END

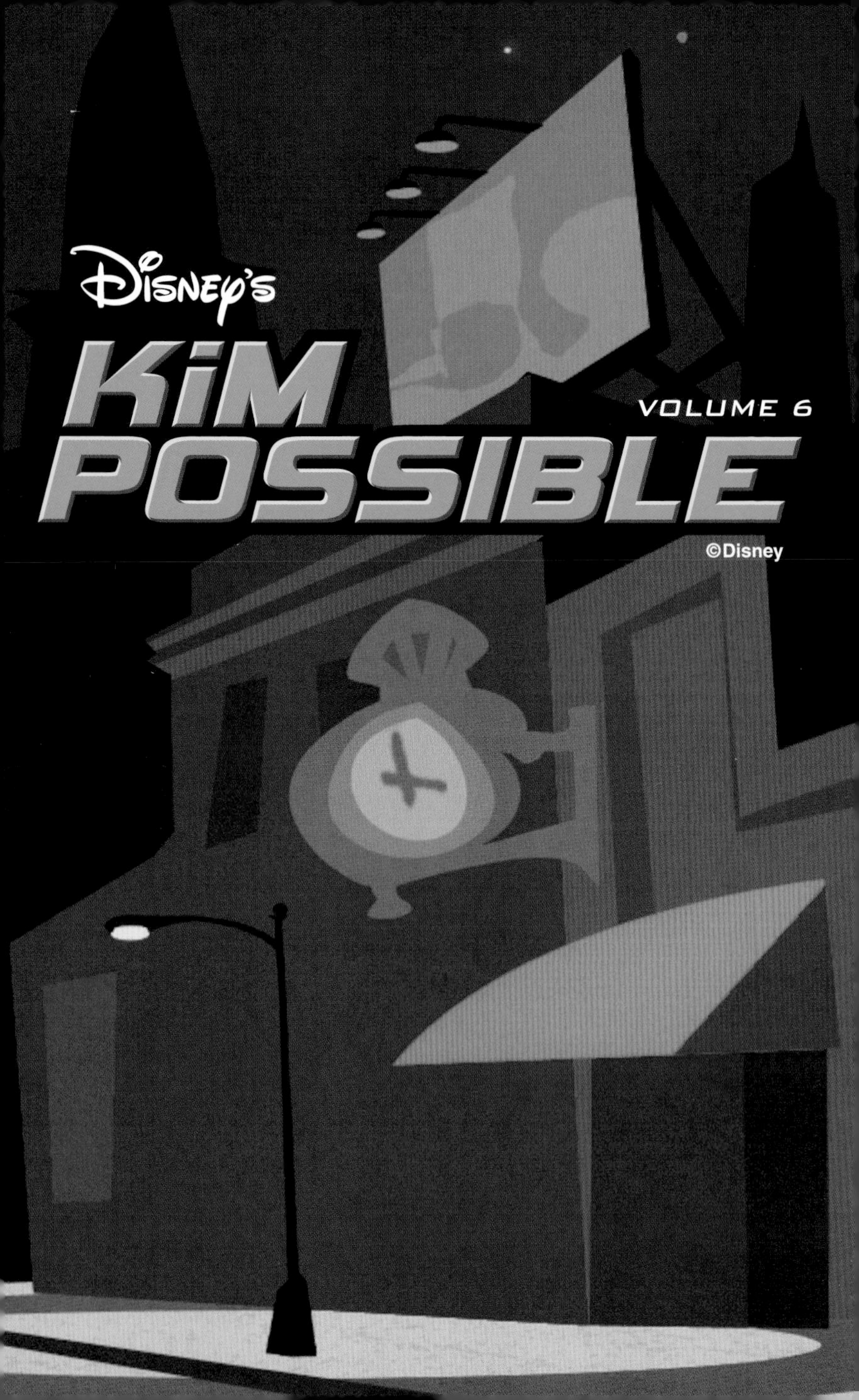

Disney's
KiM POSSIBLE
VOLUME 6
©Disney

Episode 12: Number One

Kim finds herself challenged by rivals clamoring to outdo her—both as a cheerleader and as a teen hero. With Bonnie trying to edge Kim out of the squad captain's chair and Will Du, teen agent for the Global Justice Network, trying to outmatch her crime-fighting skills, Kim needs her sidekick Ron Stoppable more than ever.

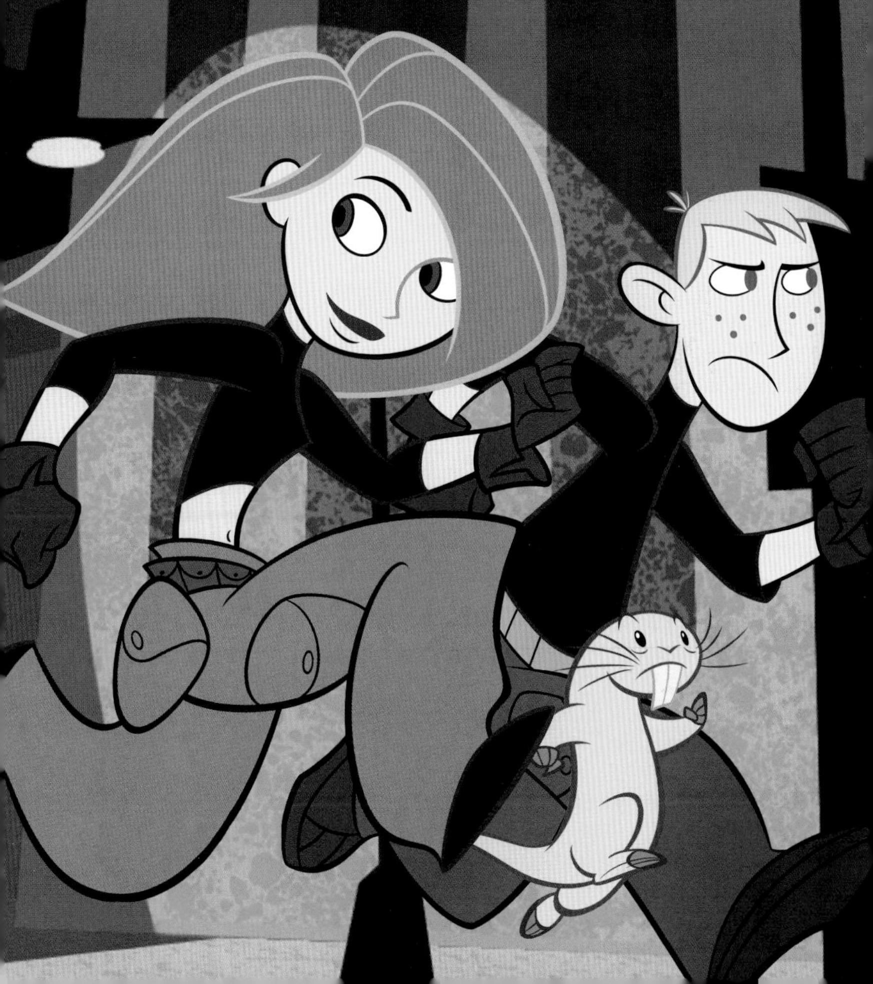

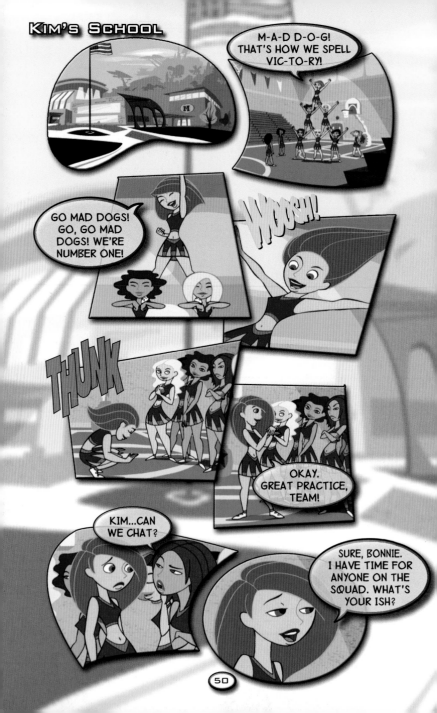

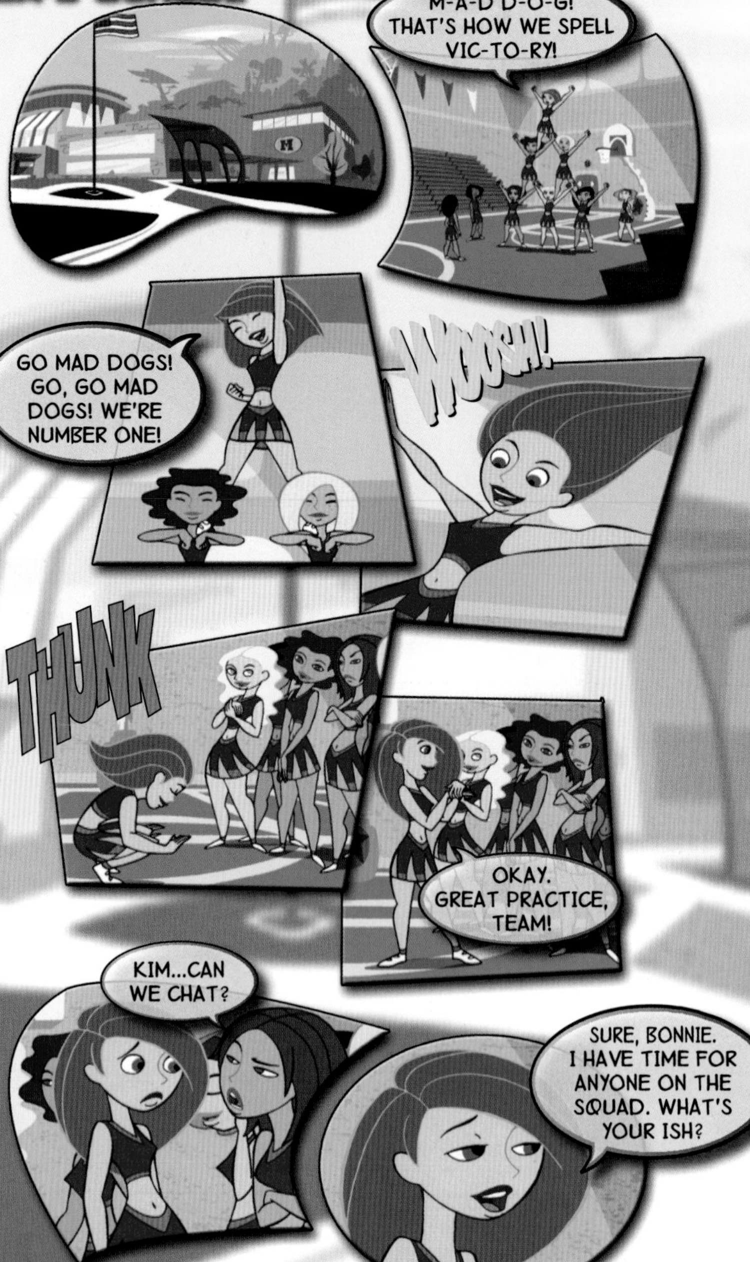
M-A-D D-O-G! THAT'S HOW WE SPELL VIC-TO-RY!
GO MAD DOGS! GO, GO MAD DOGS! WE'RE NUMBER ONE!
WHOOSH!
THUNK
OKAY. GREAT PRACTICE, TEAM!
KIM...CAN WE CHAT?
SURE, BONNIE. I HAVE TIME FOR ANYONE ON THE SQUAD. WHAT'S YOUR ISH?

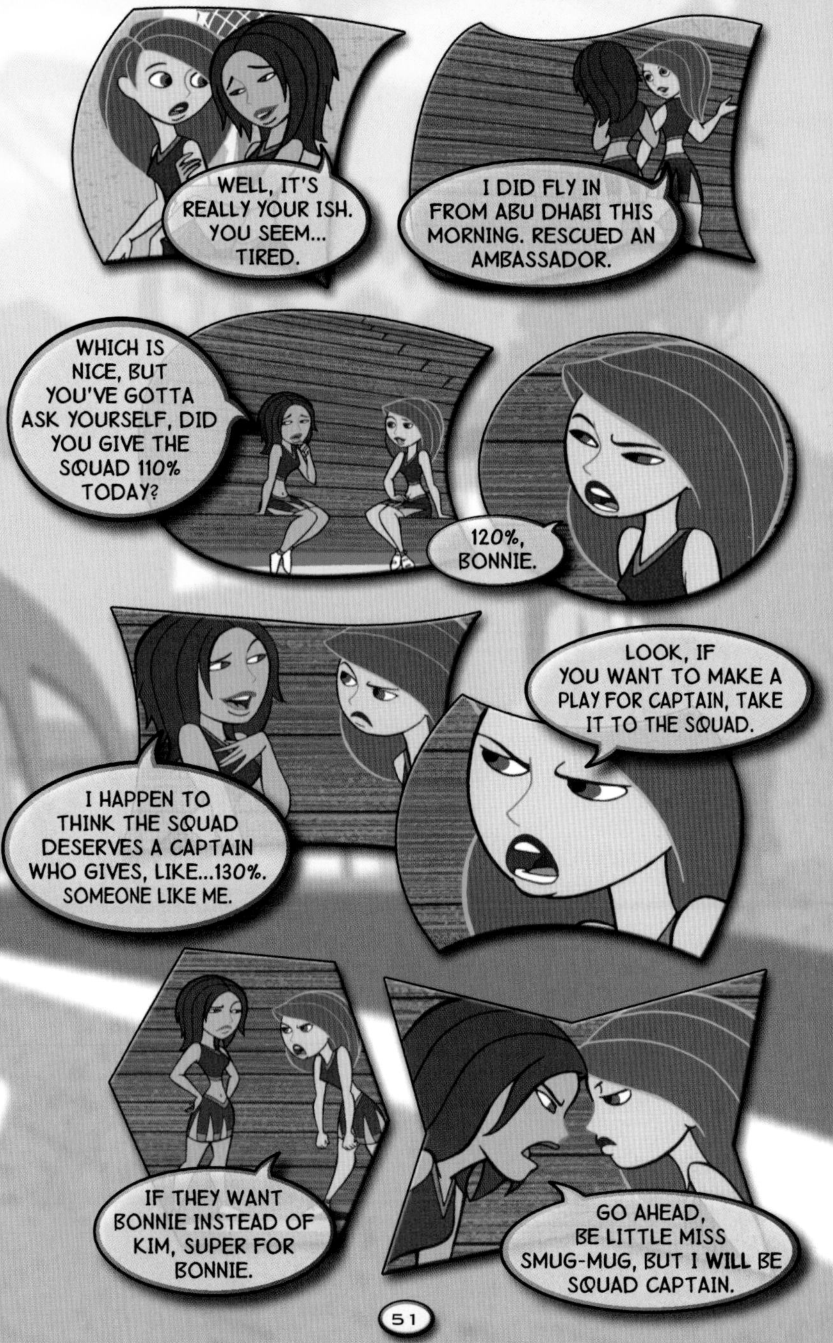
WELL, IT'S REALLY YOUR ISH. YOU SEEM... TIRED.
I DID FLY IN FROM ABU DHABI THIS MORNING. RESCUED AN AMBASSADOR.
WHICH IS NICE, BUT YOU'VE GOTTA ASK YOURSELF, DID YOU GIVE THE SQUAD 110% TODAY?
120%, BONNIE.
I HAPPEN TO THINK THE SQUAD DESERVES A CAPTAIN WHO GIVES, LIKE...130%. SOMEONE LIKE ME.
LOOK, IF YOU WANT TO MAKE A PLAY FOR CAPTAIN, TAKE IT TO THE SQUAD.
IF THEY WANT BONNIE INSTEAD OF KIM, SUPER FOR BONNIE.
GO AHEAD, BE LITTLE MISS SMUG-MUG, BUT I **WILL** BE SQUAD CAPTAIN.

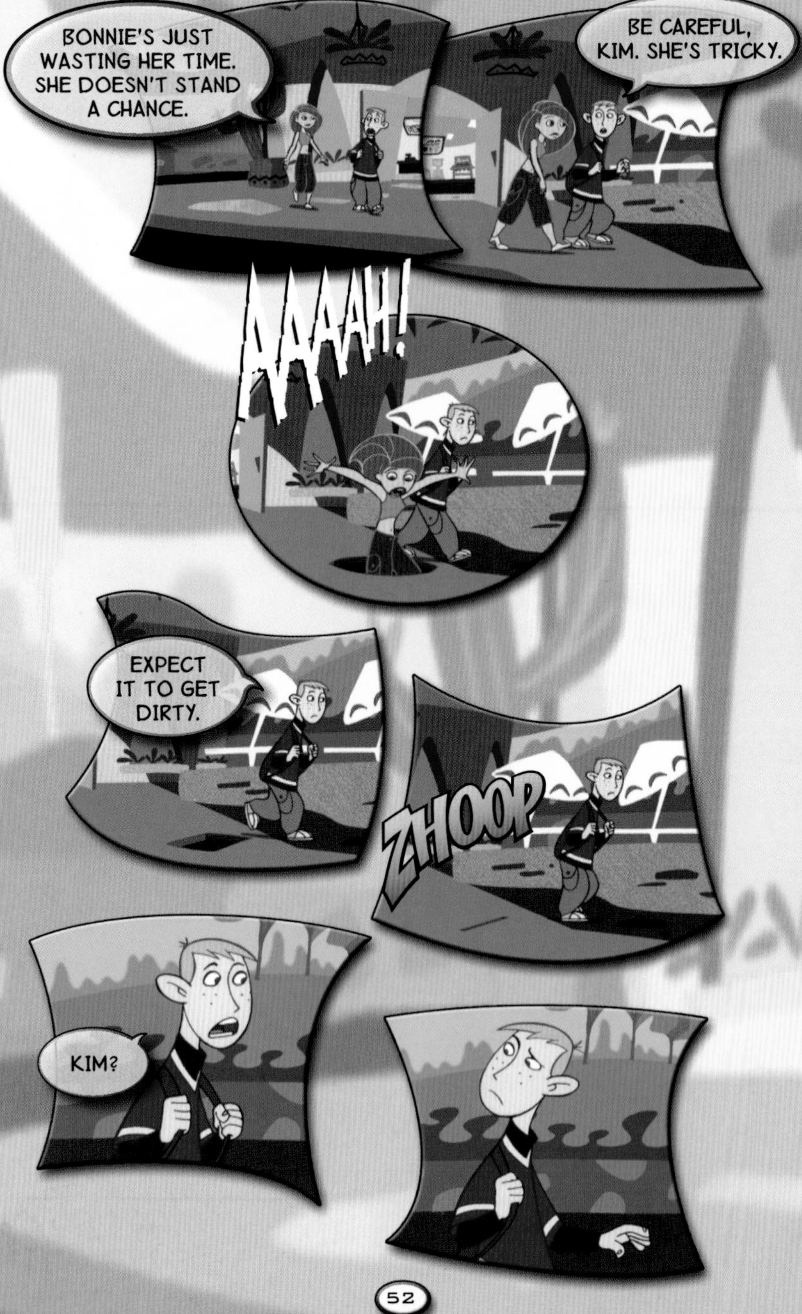
BONNIE'S JUST WASTING HER TIME. SHE DOESN'T STAND A CHANCE.
BE CAREFUL, KIM. SHE'S TRICKY.
AAAAH!
EXPECT IT TO GET DIRTY.
ZHOOP
KIM?

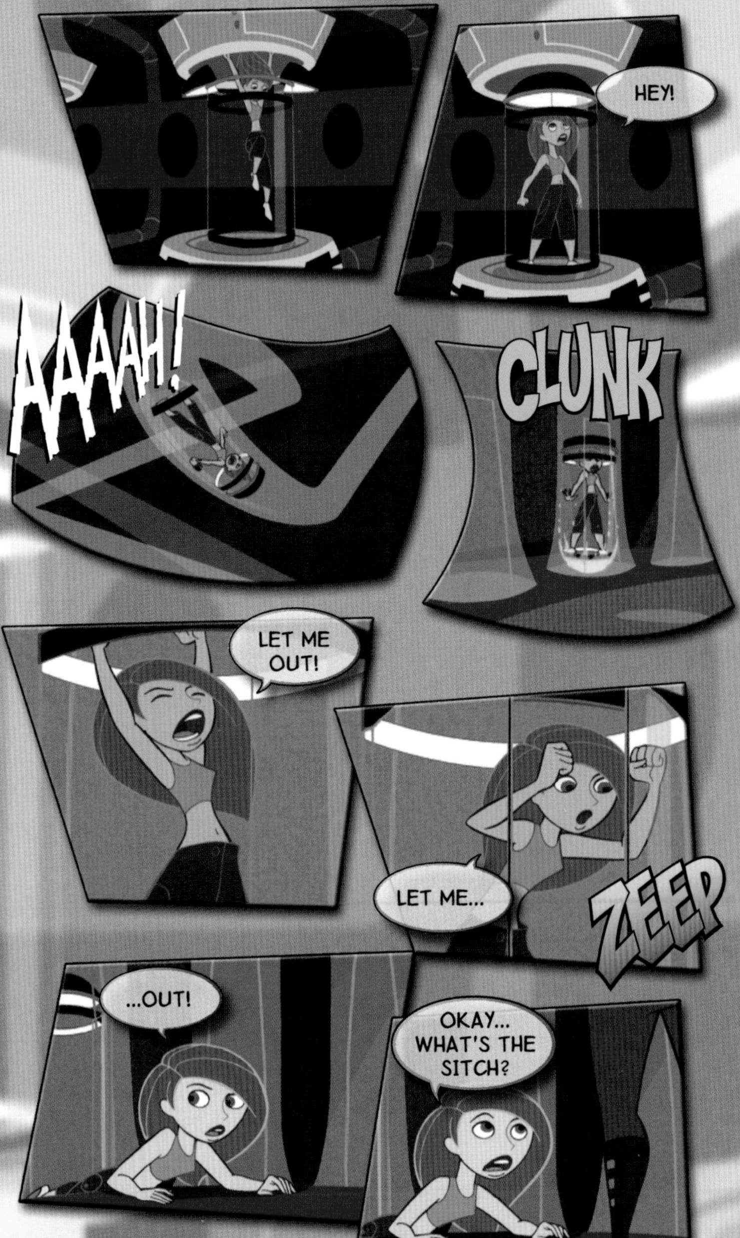
HEY!
AAAAH!
CLUNK
LET ME OUT!
LET ME...
ZEEP
...OUT!
OKAY... WHAT'S THE SITCH?

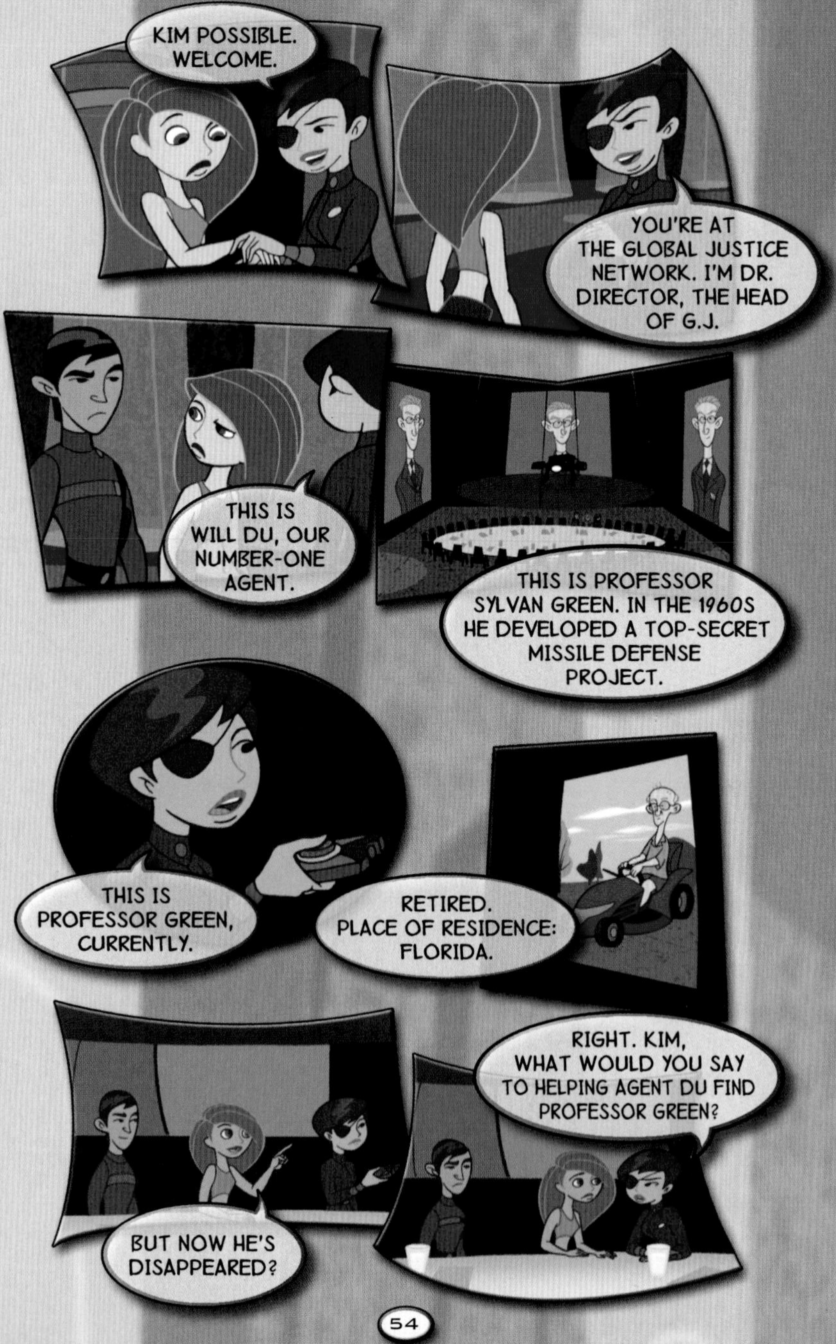
KIM POSSIBLE. WELCOME.
YOU'RE AT THE GLOBAL JUSTICE NETWORK. I'M DR. DIRECTOR, THE HEAD OF G.J.
THIS IS WILL DU, OUR NUMBER-ONE AGENT.
THIS IS PROFESSOR SYLVAN GREEN. IN THE 1960S HE DEVELOPED A TOP-SECRET MISSILE DEFENSE PROJECT.
THIS IS PROFESSOR GREEN, CURRENTLY.
RETIRED. PLACE OF RESIDENCE: FLORIDA.
BUT NOW HE'S DISAPPEARED?
RIGHT. KIM, WHAT WOULD YOU SAY TO HELPING AGENT DU FIND PROFESSOR GREEN?

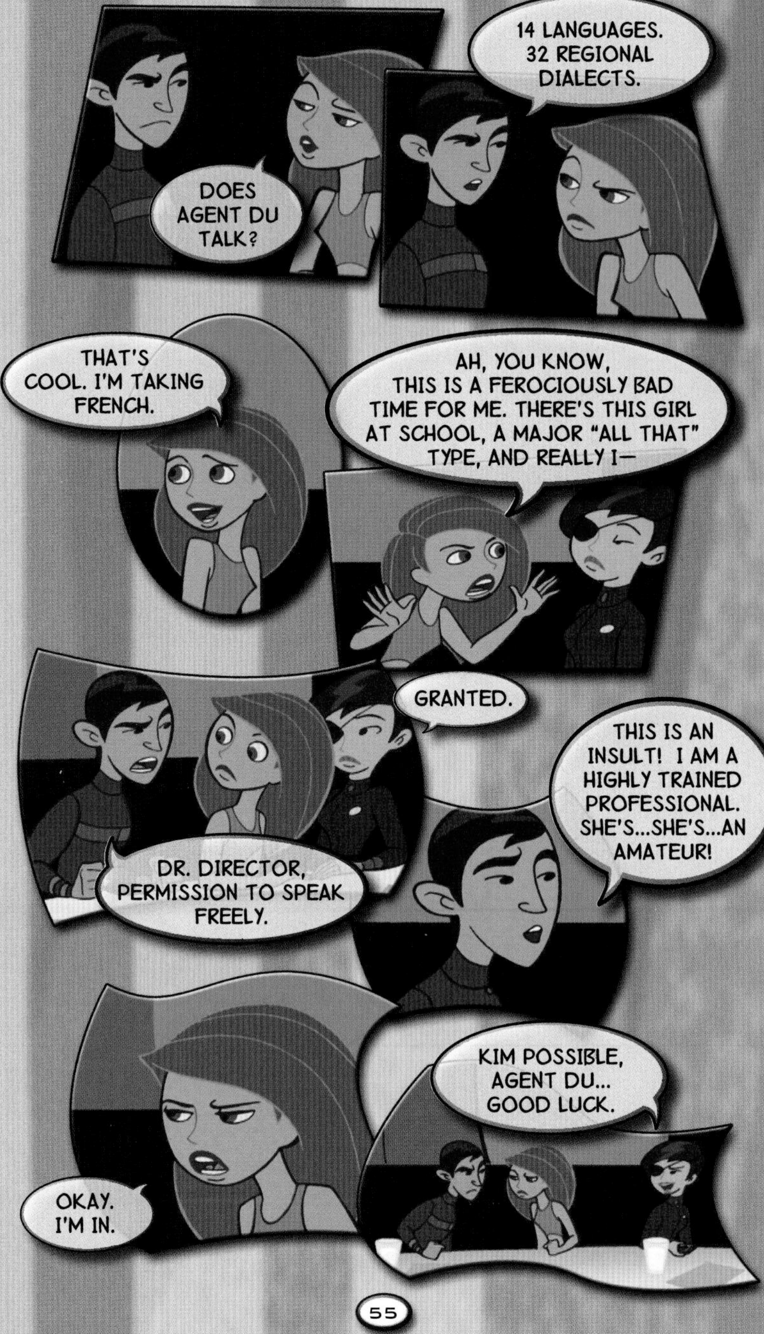
DOES AGENT DU TALK?
14 LANGUAGES. 32 REGIONAL DIALECTS.
THAT'S COOL. I'M TAKING FRENCH.
AH, YOU KNOW, THIS IS A FEROCIOUSLY BAD TIME FOR ME. THERE'S THIS GIRL AT SCHOOL, A MAJOR "ALL THAT" TYPE, AND REALLY I—
DR. DIRECTOR, PERMISSION TO SPEAK FREELY.
GRANTED.
THIS IS AN INSULT! I AM A HIGHLY TRAINED PROFESSIONAL. SHE'S...SHE'S...AN AMATEUR!
OKAY. I'M IN.
KIM POSSIBLE, AGENT DU... GOOD LUCK.

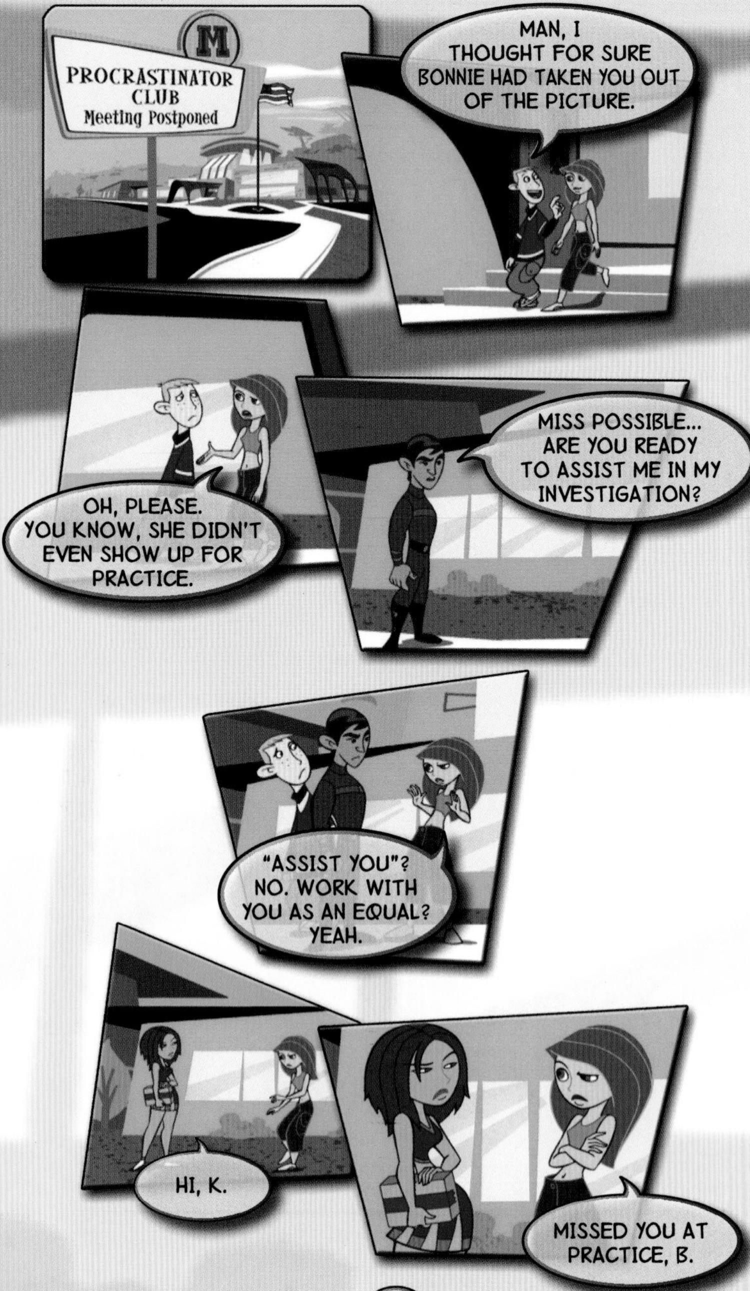
M
PROCRASTINATOR CLUB
Meeting Postponed
MAN, I THOUGHT FOR SURE BONNIE HAD TAKEN YOU OUT OF THE PICTURE.
OH, PLEASE. YOU KNOW, SHE DIDN'T EVEN SHOW UP FOR PRACTICE.
MISS POSSIBLE... ARE YOU READY TO ASSIST ME IN MY INVESTIGATION?
"ASSIST YOU"? NO. WORK WITH YOU AS AN EQUAL? YEAH.
HI, K.
MISSED YOU AT PRACTICE, B.

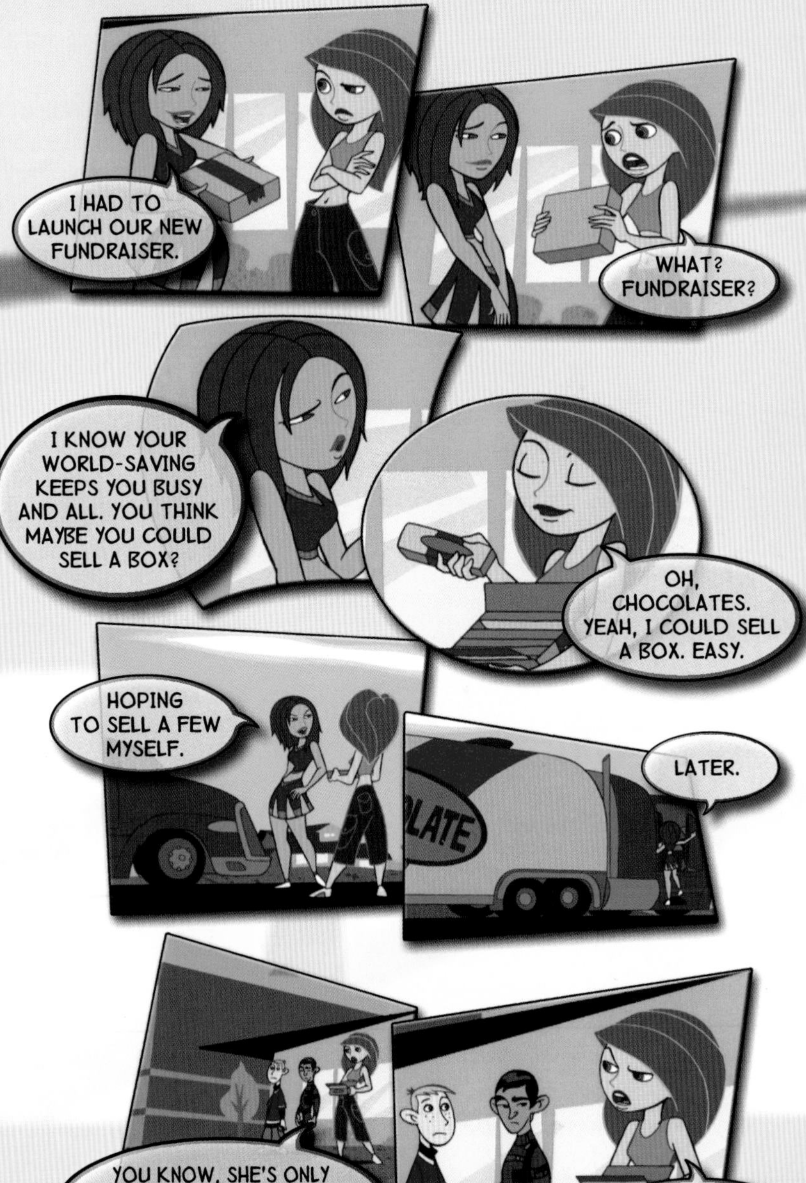
I HAD TO LAUNCH OUR NEW FUNDRAISER.
WHAT? FUNDRAISER?
I KNOW YOUR WORLD-SAVING KEEPS YOU BUSY AND ALL. YOU THINK MAYBE YOU COULD SELL A BOX?
OH, CHOCOLATES. YEAH, I COULD SELL A BOX. EASY.
HOPING TO SELL A FEW MYSELF.
LATER.
OLATE
YOU KNOW, SHE'S ONLY KIDDING HERSELF. THERE IS NO WAY SHE'S GONNA SELL ALL THAT.
LET'S JUST GET ON WITH THE MISSION.

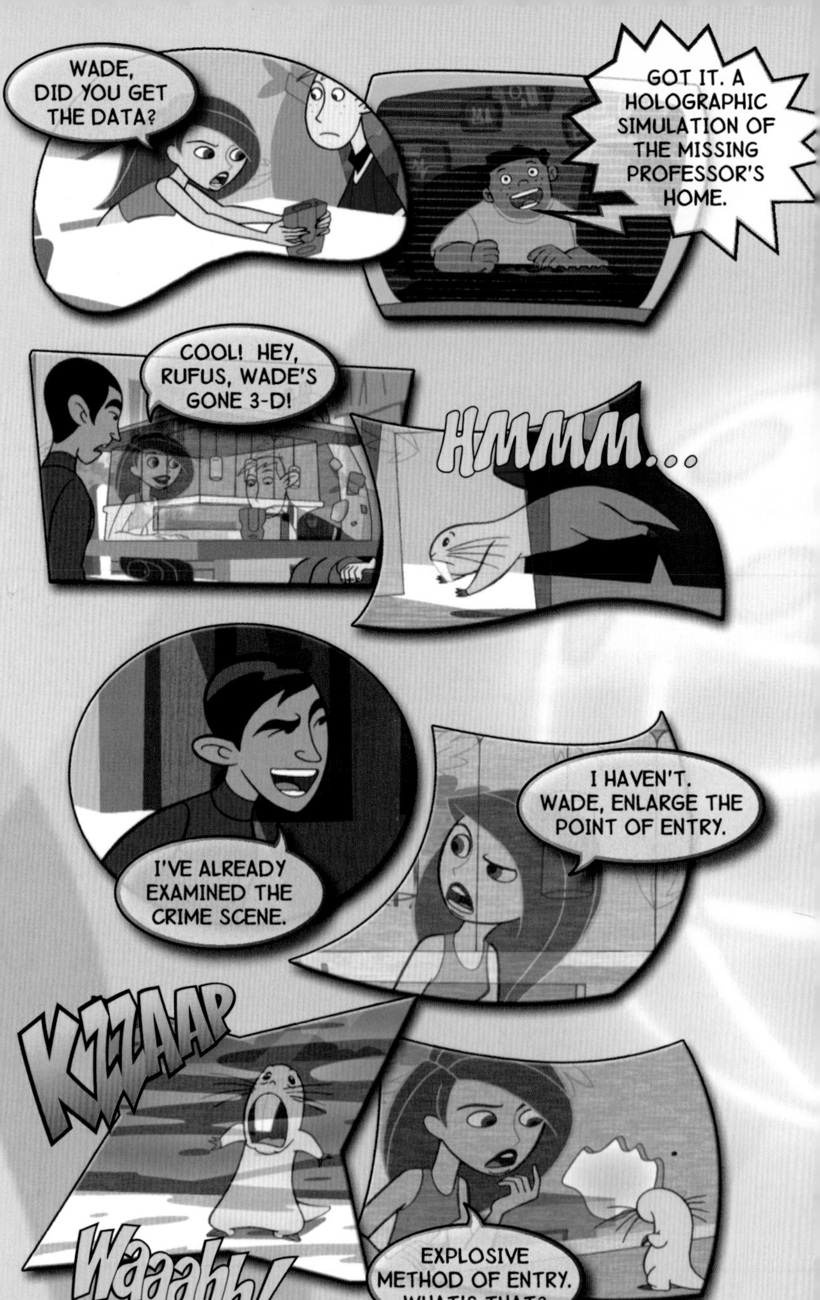
WADE, DID YOU GET THE DATA?
GOT IT. A HOLOGRAPHIC SIMULATION OF THE MISSING PROFESSOR'S HOME.
COOL! HEY, RUFUS, WADE'S GONE 3-D!
HMMM...
I'VE ALREADY EXAMINED THE CRIME SCENE.
I HAVEN'T. WADE, ENLARGE THE POINT OF ENTRY.
KZZAAP
Waaahh!
EXPLOSIVE METHOD OF ENTRY. WHAT'S THAT?

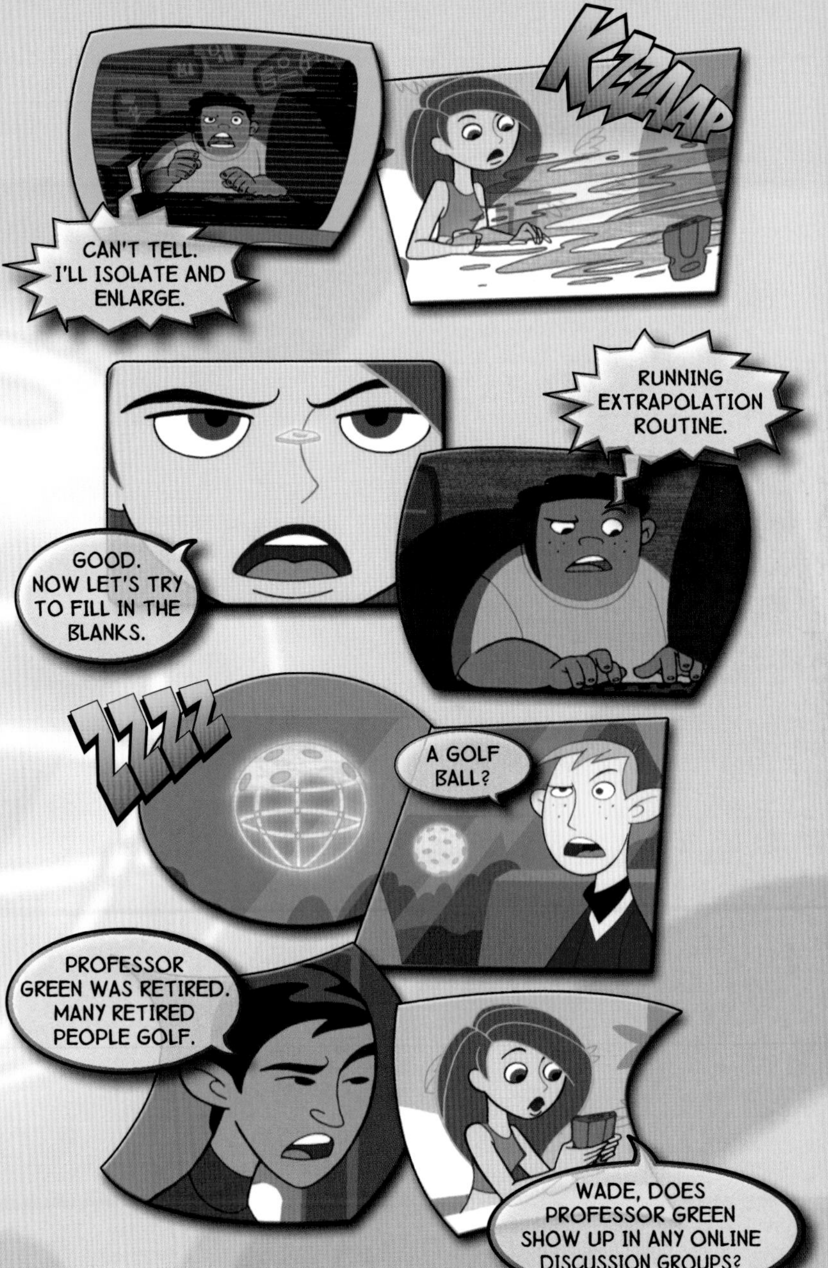
CAN'T TELL. I'LL ISOLATE AND ENLARGE.
KZZAAP
RUNNING EXTRAPOLATION ROUTINE.
GOOD. NOW LET'S TRY TO FILL IN THE BLANKS.
ZZZZ
A GOLF BALL?
PROFESSOR GREEN WAS RETIRED. MANY RETIRED PEOPLE GOLF.
WADE, DOES PROFESSOR GREEN SHOW UP IN ANY ONLINE DISCUSSION GROUPS?

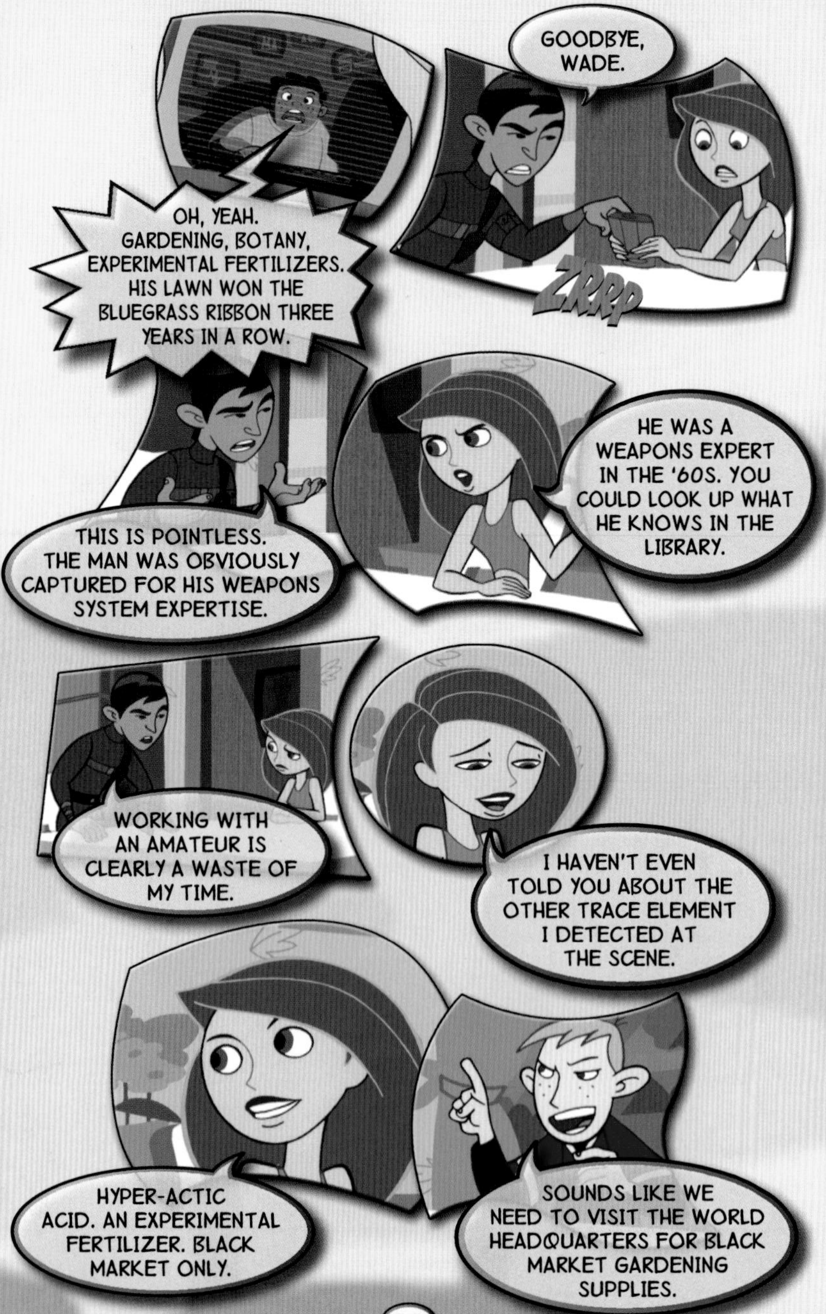
OH, YEAH. GARDENING, BOTANY, EXPERIMENTAL FERTILIZERS. HIS LAWN WON THE BLUEGRASS RIBBON THREE YEARS IN A ROW.
GOODBYE, WADE.
ZRRP
THIS IS POINTLESS. THE MAN WAS OBVIOUSLY CAPTURED FOR HIS WEAPONS SYSTEM EXPERTISE.
HE WAS A WEAPONS EXPERT IN THE '60S. YOU COULD LOOK UP WHAT HE KNOWS IN THE LIBRARY.
WORKING WITH AN AMATEUR IS CLEARLY A WASTE OF MY TIME.
I HAVEN'T EVEN TOLD YOU ABOUT THE OTHER TRACE ELEMENT I DETECTED AT THE SCENE.
HYPER-ACTIC ACID. AN EXPERIMENTAL FERTILIZER. BLACK MARKET ONLY.
SOUNDS LIKE WE NEED TO VISIT THE WORLD HEADQUARTERS FOR BLACK MARKET GARDENING SUPPLIES.

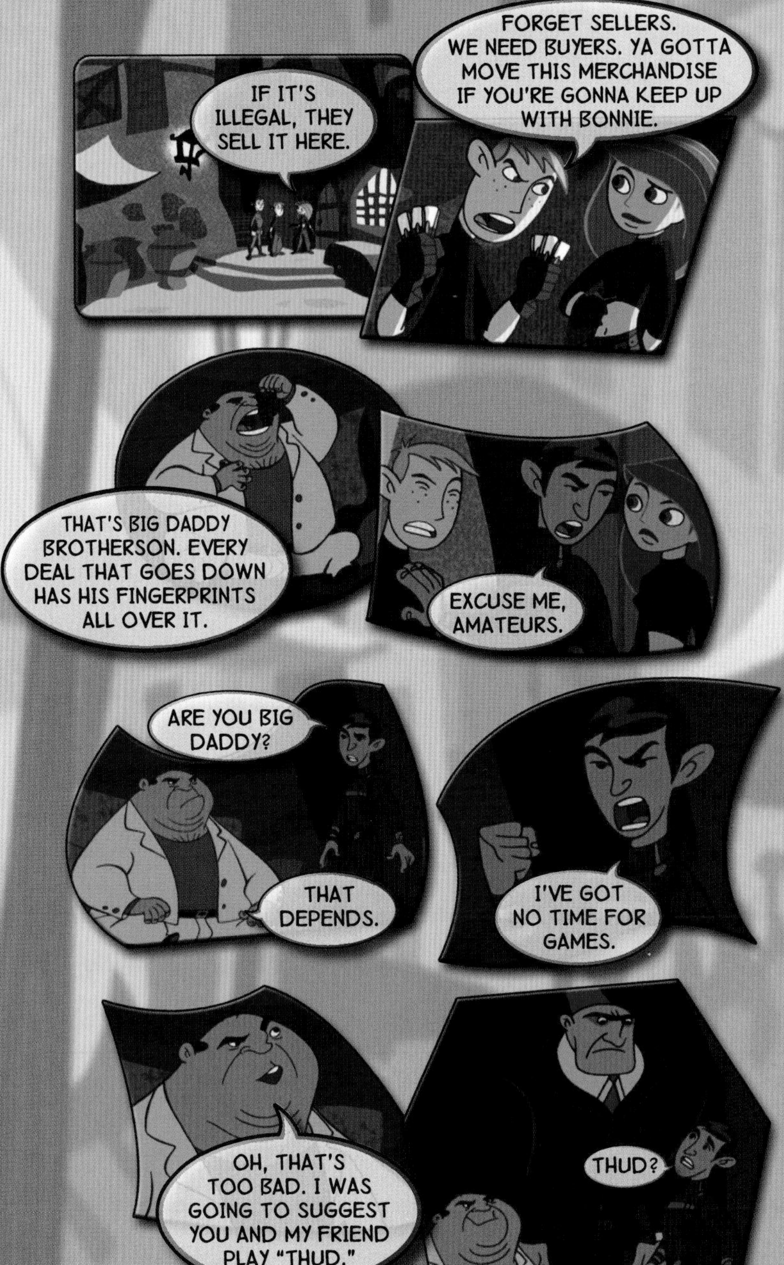
IF IT'S ILLEGAL, THEY SELL IT HERE.
FORGET SELLERS. WE NEED BUYERS. YA GOTTA MOVE THIS MERCHANDISE IF YOU'RE GONNA KEEP UP WITH BONNIE.
THAT'S BIG DADDY BROTHERSON. EVERY DEAL THAT GOES DOWN HAS HIS FINGERPRINTS ALL OVER IT.
EXCUSE ME, AMATEURS.
ARE YOU BIG DADDY?
THAT DEPENDS.
I'VE GOT NO TIME FOR GAMES.
OH, THAT'S TOO BAD. I WAS GOING TO SUGGEST YOU AND MY FRIEND PLAY "THUD."
THUD?

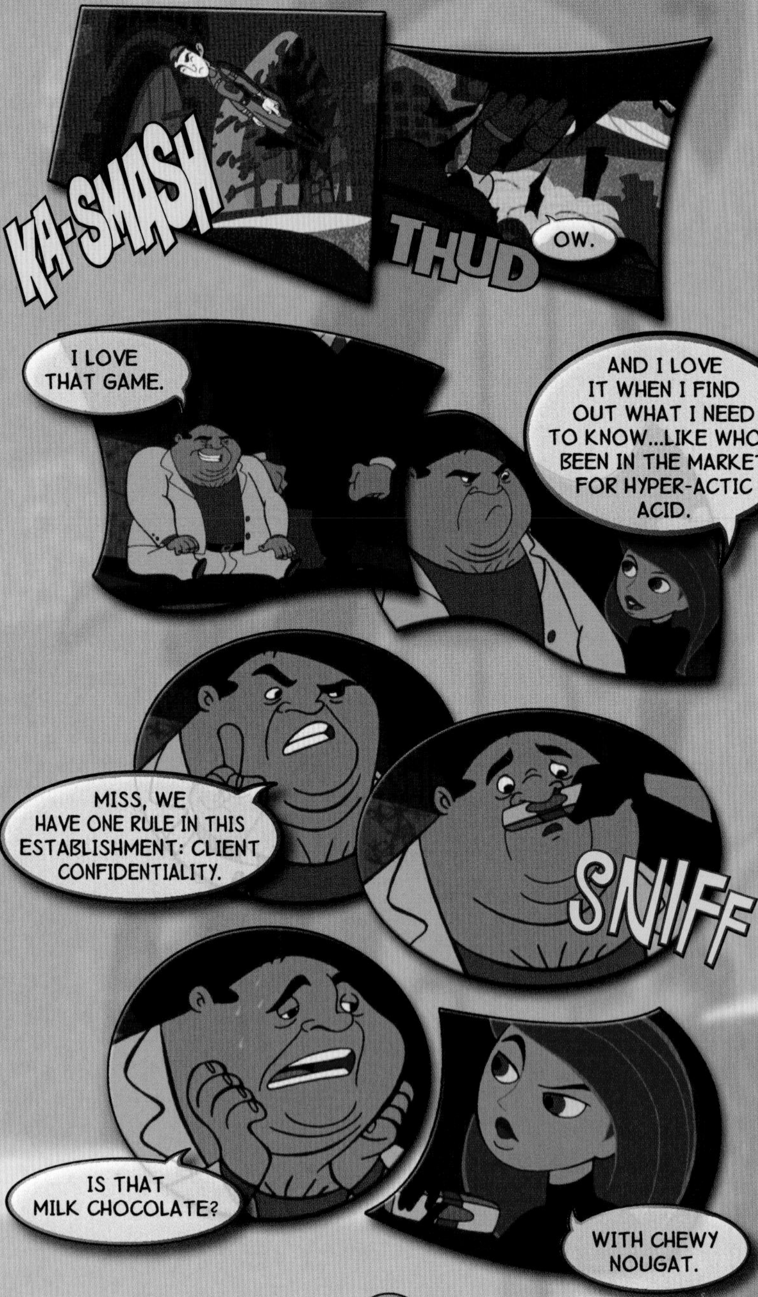
KA-SMASH
THUD
OW.
I LOVE THAT GAME.
AND I LOVE IT WHEN I FIND OUT WHAT I NEED TO KNOW...LIKE WHO'S BEEN IN THE MARKET FOR HYPER-ACTIC ACID.
MISS, WE HAVE ONE RULE IN THIS ESTABLISHMENT: CLIENT CONFIDENTIALITY.
SNIFF
IS THAT MILK CHOCOLATE?
WITH CHEWY NOUGAT.

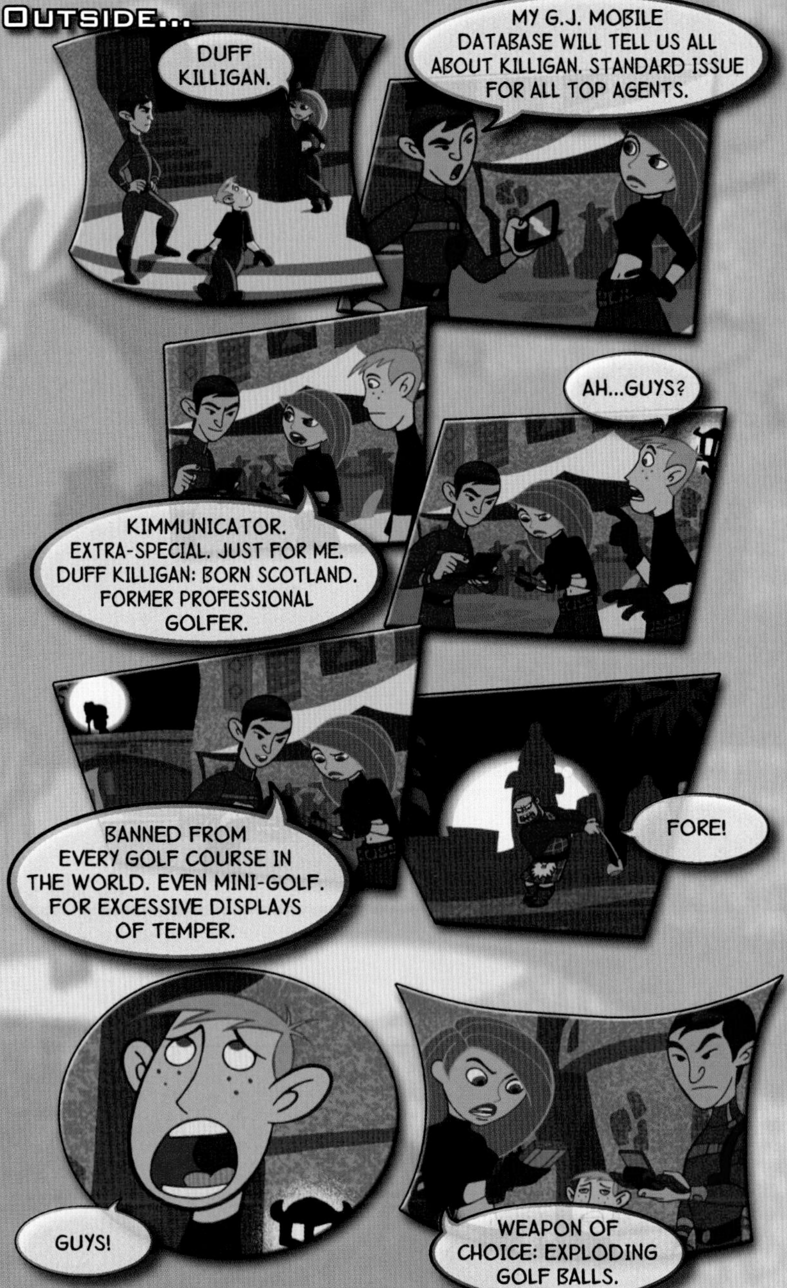
OUTSIDE...
DUFF KILLIGAN.
MY G.J. MOBILE DATABASE WILL TELL US ALL ABOUT KILLIGAN. STANDARD ISSUE FOR ALL TOP AGENTS.
KIMMUNICATOR. EXTRA-SPECIAL. JUST FOR ME. DUFF KILLIGAN: BORN SCOTLAND. FORMER PROFESSIONAL GOLFER.
AH...GUYS?
BANNED FROM EVERY GOLF COURSE IN THE WORLD. EVEN MINI-GOLF. FOR EXCESSIVE DISPLAYS OF TEMPER.
FORE!
GUYS!
WEAPON OF CHOICE: EXPLODING GOLF BALLS.

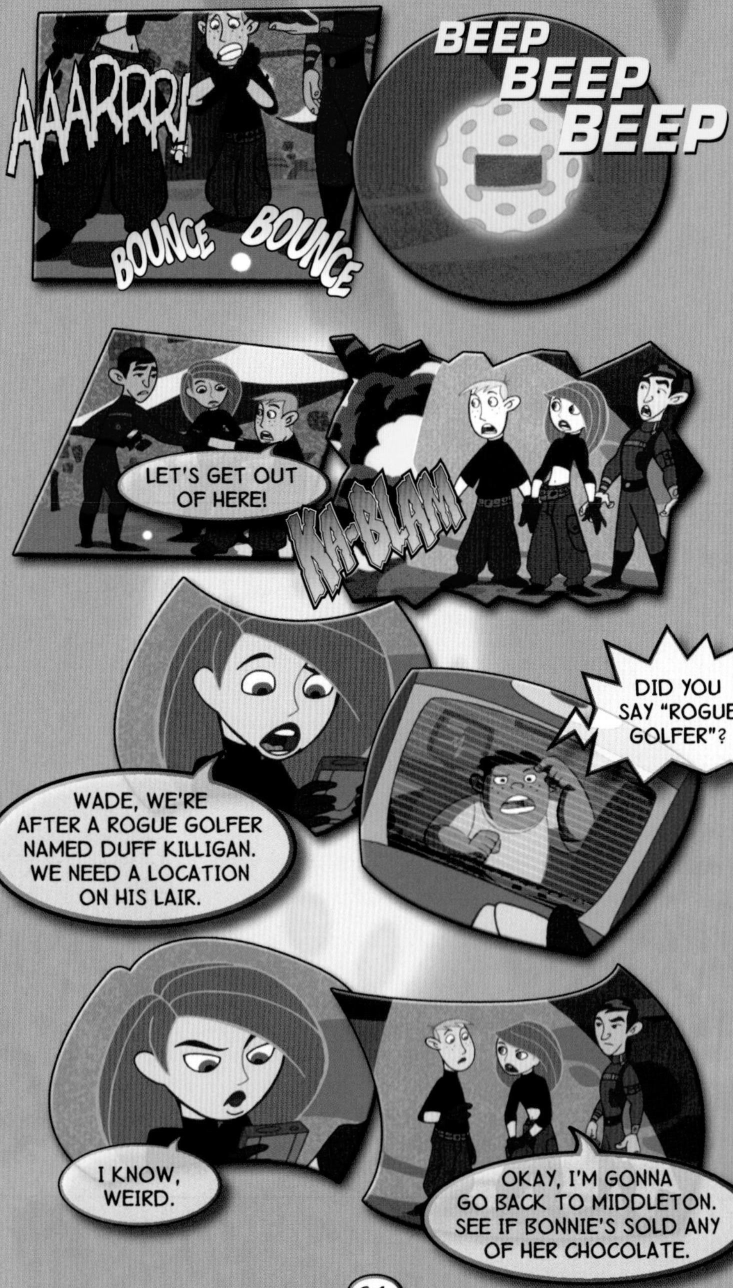
AAARRR!
BOUNCE
BOUNCE
BEEP
BEEP
BEEP
LET'S GET OUT OF HERE!
KA-BLAM
WADE, WE'RE AFTER A ROGUE GOLFER NAMED DUFF KILLIGAN. WE NEED A LOCATION ON HIS LAIR.
DID YOU SAY "ROGUE GOLFER"?
I KNOW, WEIRD.
OKAY, I'M GONNA GO BACK TO MIDDLETON. SEE IF BONNIE'S SOLD ANY OF HER CHOCOLATE.

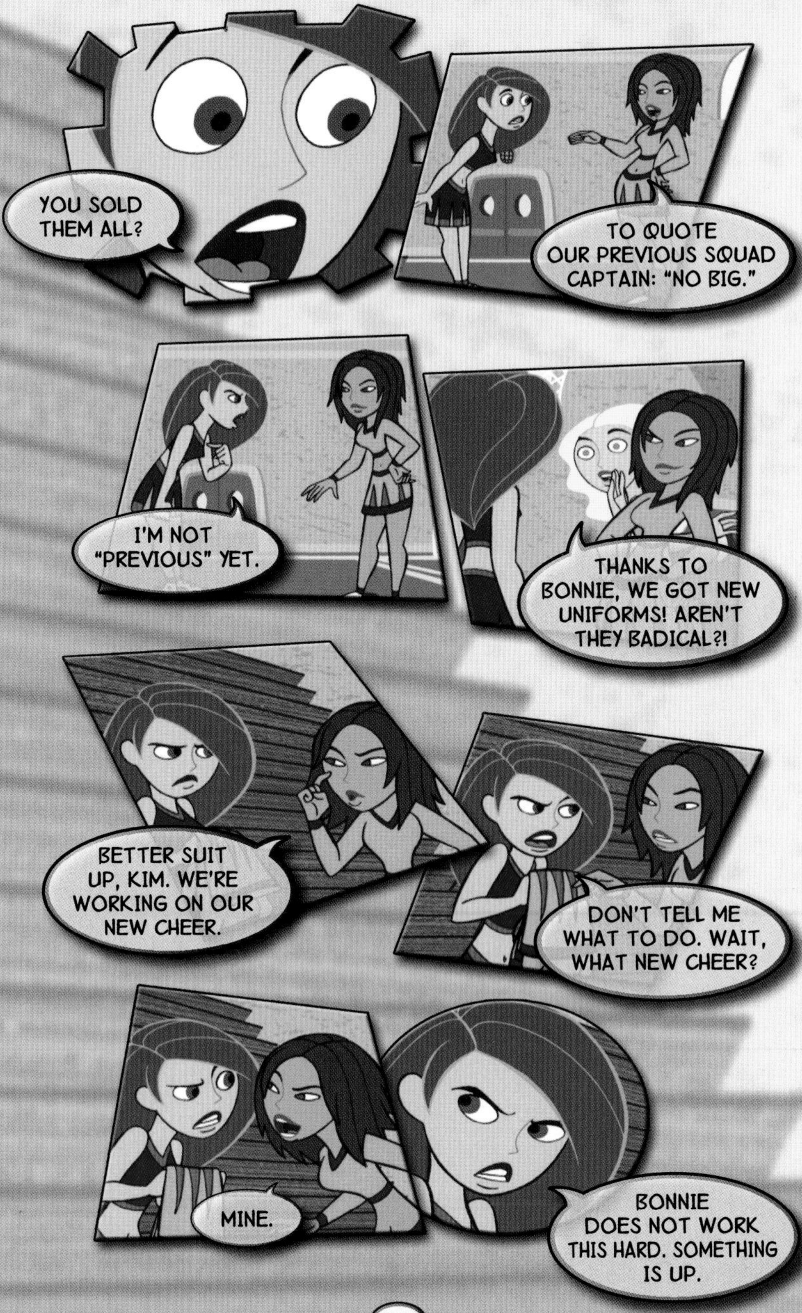
YOU SOLD THEM ALL?
TO QUOTE OUR PREVIOUS SQUAD CAPTAIN: "NO BIG."
I'M NOT "PREVIOUS" YET.
THANKS TO BONNIE, WE GOT NEW UNIFORMS! AREN'T THEY BADICAL?!
BETTER SUIT UP, KIM. WE'RE WORKING ON OUR NEW CHEER.
DON'T TELL ME WHAT TO DO. WAIT, WHAT NEW CHEER?
MINE.
BONNIE DOES NOT WORK THIS HARD. SOMETHING IS UP.

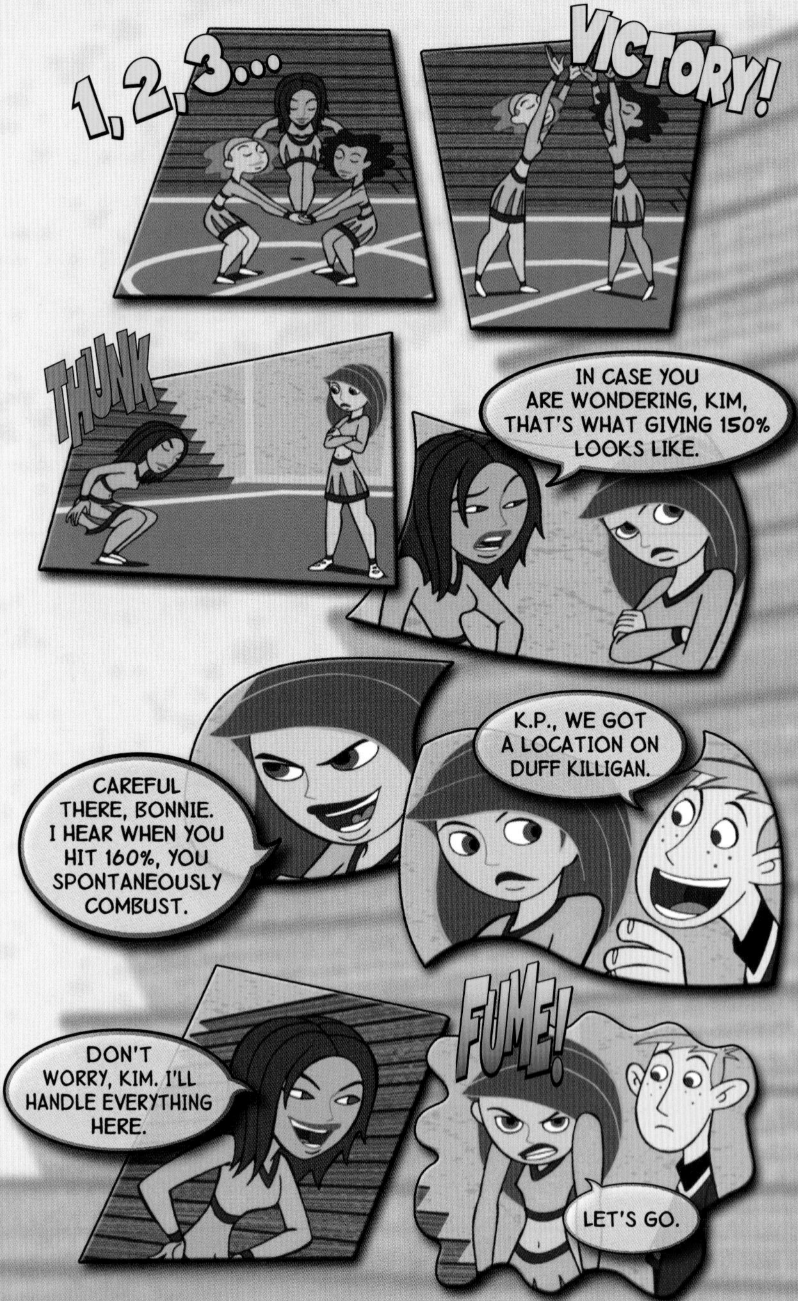
1, 2, 3...
VICTORY!
THUNK
IN CASE YOU ARE WONDERING, KIM, THAT'S WHAT GIVING 150% LOOKS LIKE.
CAREFUL THERE, BONNIE. I HEAR WHEN YOU HIT 160%, YOU SPONTANEOUSLY COMBUST.
K.P., WE GOT A LOCATION ON DUFF KILLIGAN.
DON'T WORRY, KIM. I'LL HANDLE EVERYTHING HERE.
FUME!
LET'S GO.

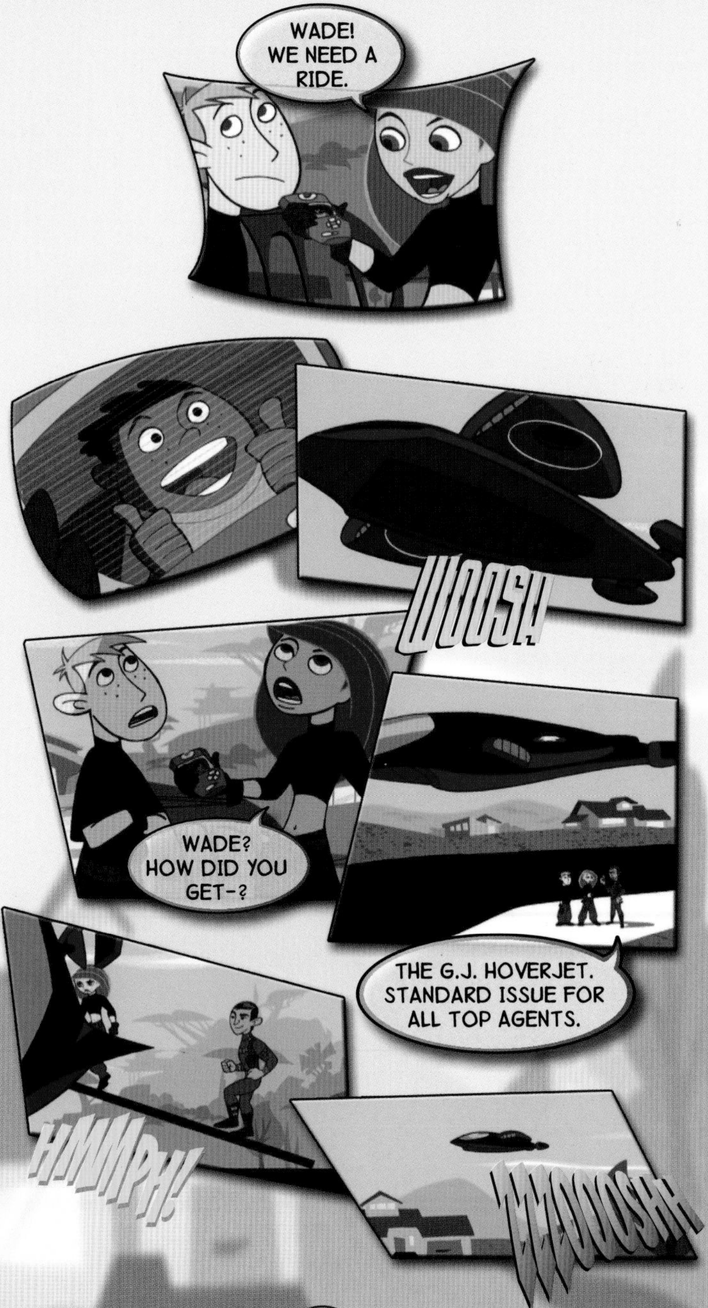
WADE! WE NEED A RIDE.
WOOSH
WADE? HOW DID YOU GET-?
THE G.J. HOVERJET. STANDARD ISSUE FOR ALL TOP AGENTS.
HMMPH!
WOOOSH

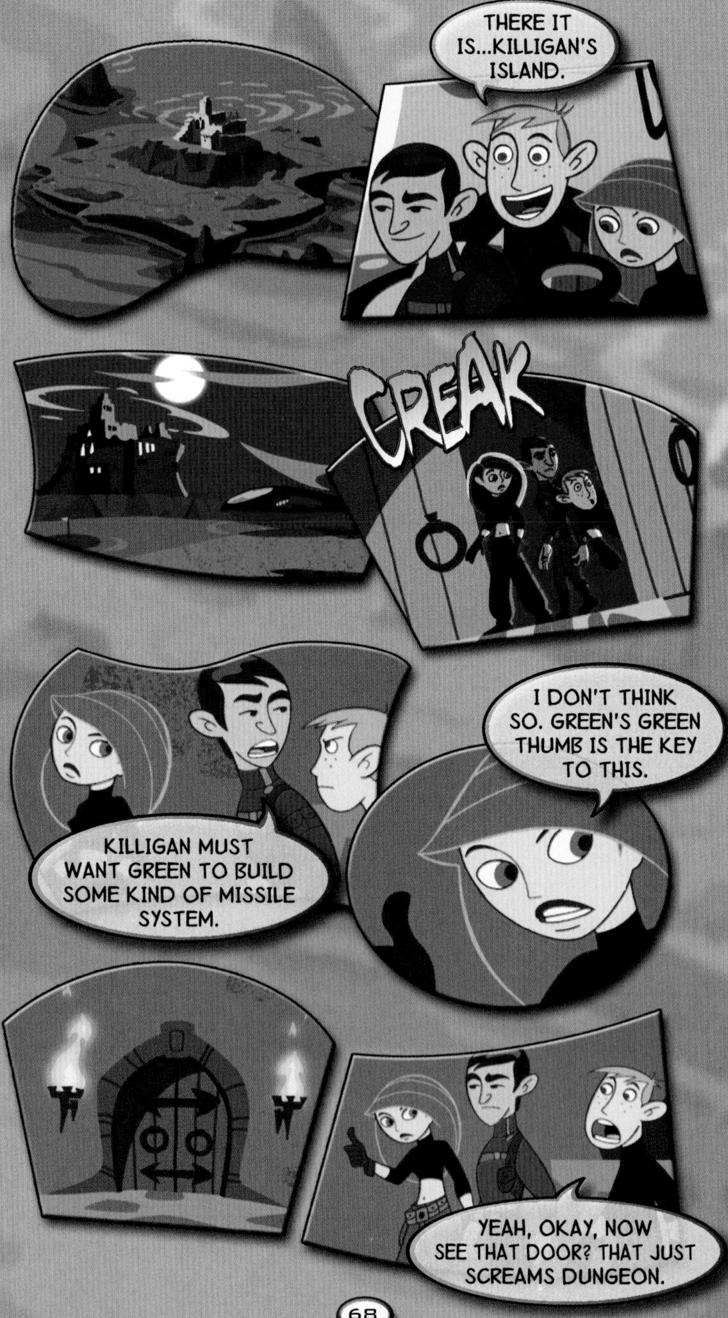
THERE IT IS...KILLIGAN'S ISLAND.
CREAK
KILLIGAN MUST WANT GREEN TO BUILD SOME KIND OF MISSILE SYSTEM.
I DON'T THINK SO. GREEN'S GREEN THUMB IS THE KEY TO THIS.
YEAH, OKAY, NOW SEE THAT DOOR? THAT JUST SCREAMS DUNGEON.

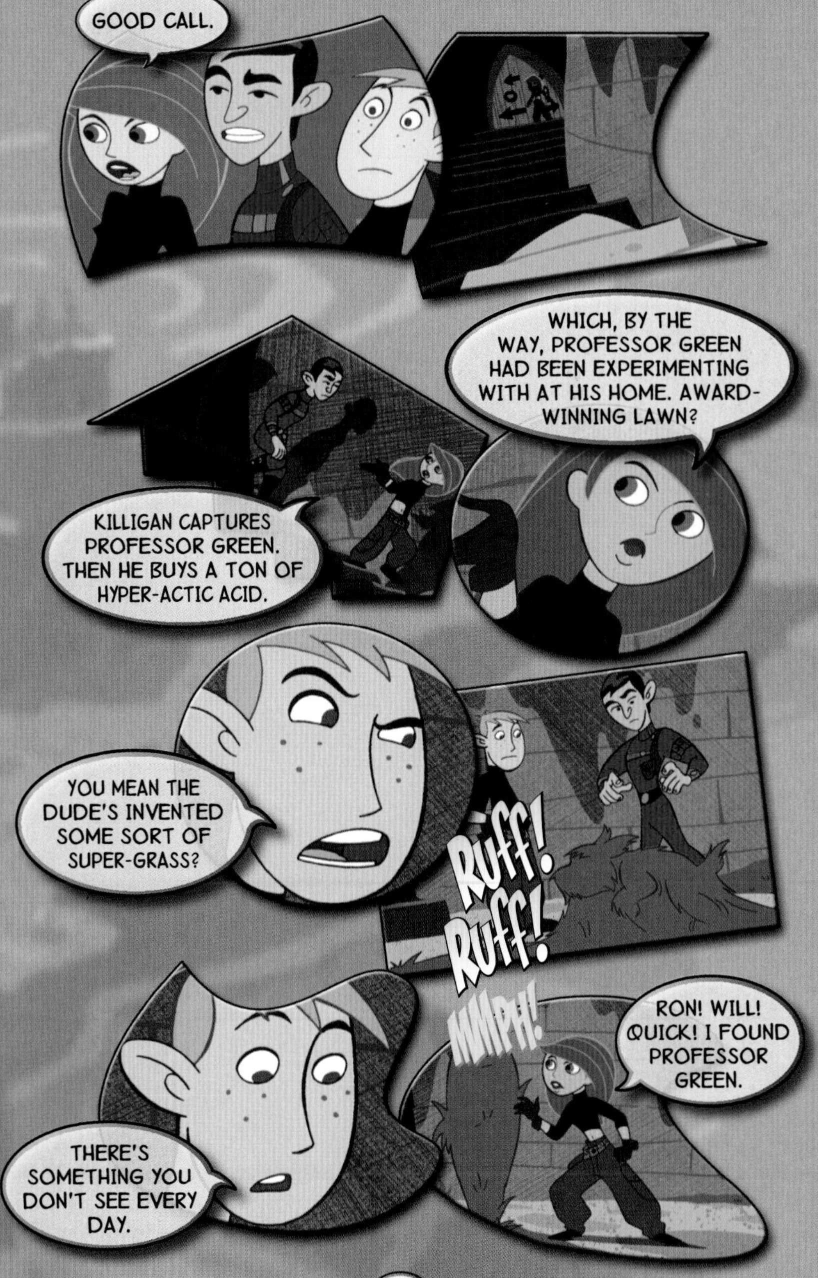
GOOD CALL.
WHICH, BY THE WAY, PROFESSOR GREEN HAD BEEN EXPERIMENTING WITH AT HIS HOME. AWARD-WINNING LAWN?
KILLIGAN CAPTURES PROFESSOR GREEN. THEN HE BUYS A TON OF HYPER-ACTIC ACID.
YOU MEAN THE DUDE'S INVENTED SOME SORT OF SUPER-GRASS?
RUFF! RUFF!
MMPH!
RON! WILL! QUICK! I FOUND PROFESSOR GREEN.
THERE'S SOMETHING YOU DON'T SEE EVERY DAY.

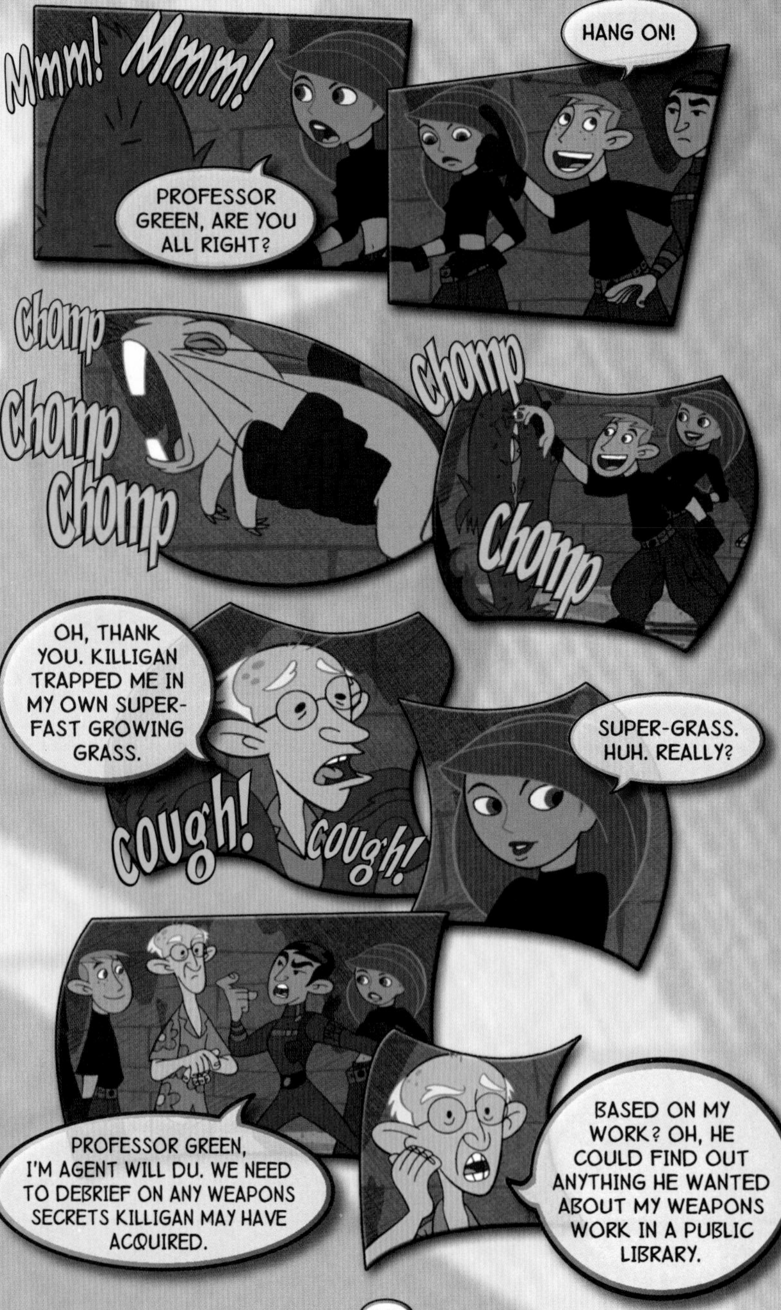

Mmm! Mmm!
PROFESSOR GREEN, ARE YOU ALL RIGHT?
HANG ON!
Chomp
Chomp
Chomp
Chomp
Chomp
OH, THANK YOU. KILLIGAN TRAPPED ME IN MY OWN SUPER-FAST GROWING GRASS.
cough! cough!
SUPER-GRASS. HUH. REALLY?
PROFESSOR GREEN, I'M AGENT WILL DU. WE NEED TO DEBRIEF ON ANY WEAPONS SECRETS KILLIGAN MAY HAVE ACQUIRED.
BASED ON MY WORK? OH, HE COULD FIND OUT ANYTHING HE WANTED ABOUT MY WEAPONS WORK IN A PUBLIC LIBRARY.

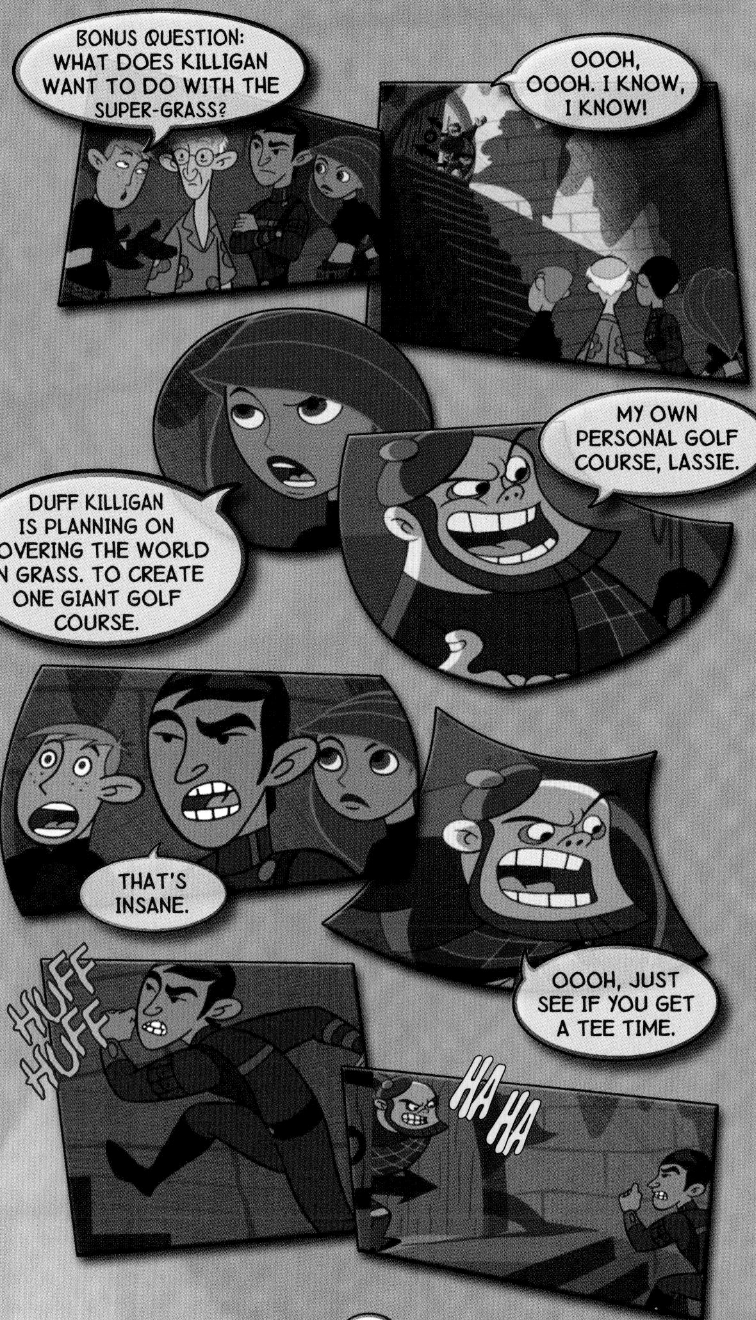
BONUS QUESTION: WHAT DOES KILLIGAN WANT TO DO WITH THE SUPER-GRASS?
OOOH, OOOH. I KNOW, I KNOW!
DUFF KILLIGAN IS PLANNING ON COVERING THE WORLD IN GRASS. TO CREATE ONE GIANT GOLF COURSE.
MY OWN PERSONAL GOLF COURSE, LASSIE.
THAT'S INSANE.
OOOH, JUST SEE IF YOU GET A TEE TIME.
HUFF HUFF
HA HA

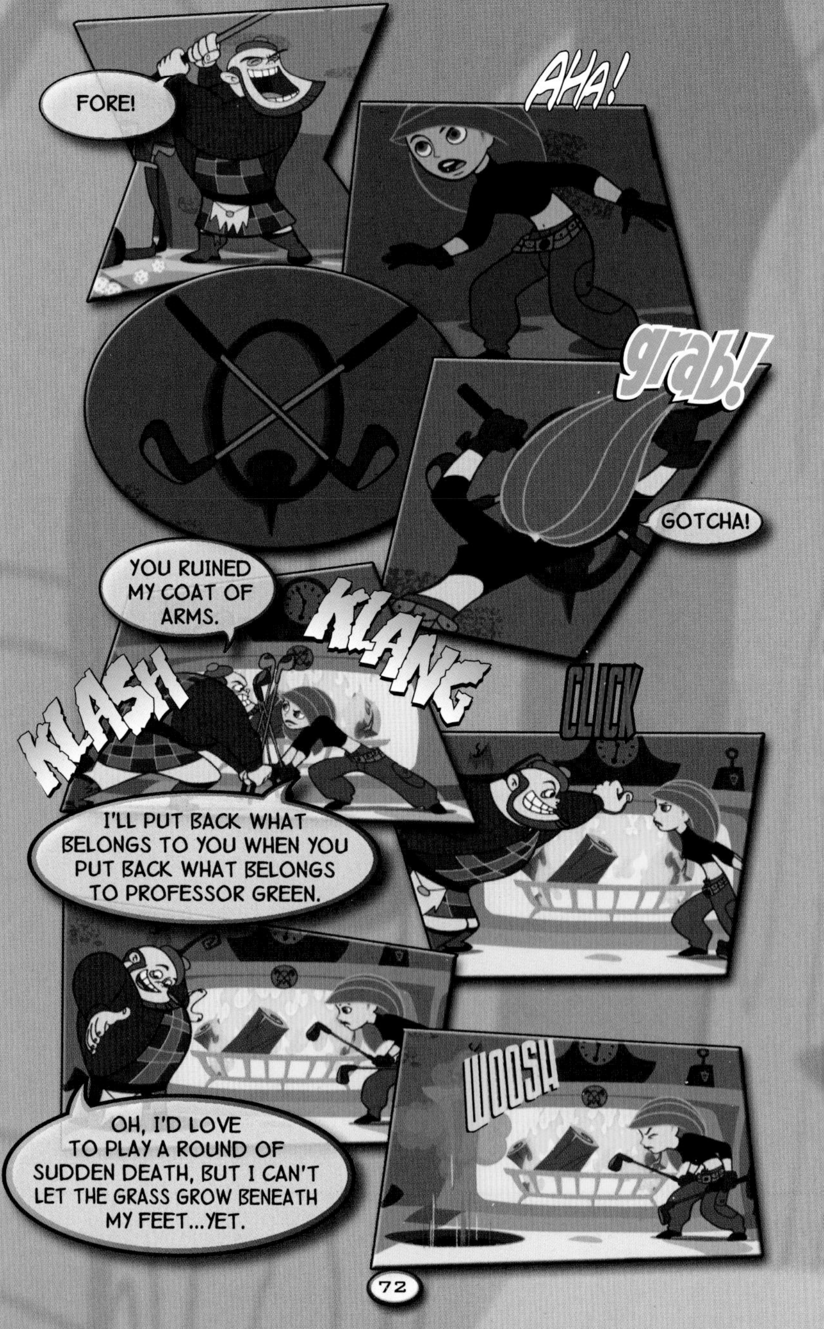
FORE!
AHA!
grab!
GOTCHA!
YOU RUINED MY COAT OF ARMS.
KLANG
KLASH
CLICK
I'LL PUT BACK WHAT BELONGS TO YOU WHEN YOU PUT BACK WHAT BELONGS TO PROFESSOR GREEN.
OH, I'D LOVE TO PLAY A ROUND OF SUDDEN DEATH, BUT I CAN'T LET THE GRASS GROW BENEATH MY FEET...YET.
WOOSH

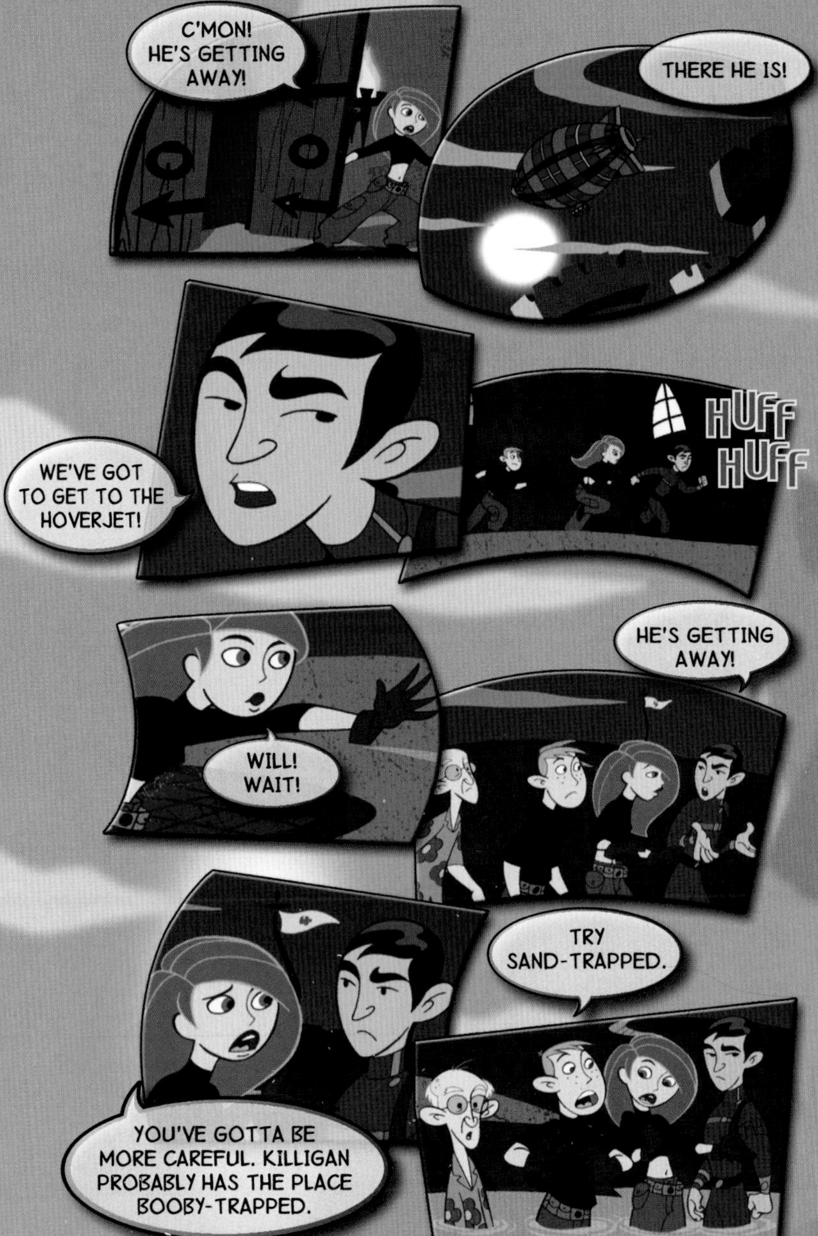
C'MON! HE'S GETTING AWAY!
THERE HE IS!
WE'VE GOT TO GET TO THE HOVERJET!
HUFF HUFF
WILL! WAIT!
HE'S GETTING AWAY!
YOU'VE GOTTA BE MORE CAREFUL. KILLIGAN PROBABLY HAS THE PLACE BOOBY-TRAPPED.
TRY SAND-TRAPPED.

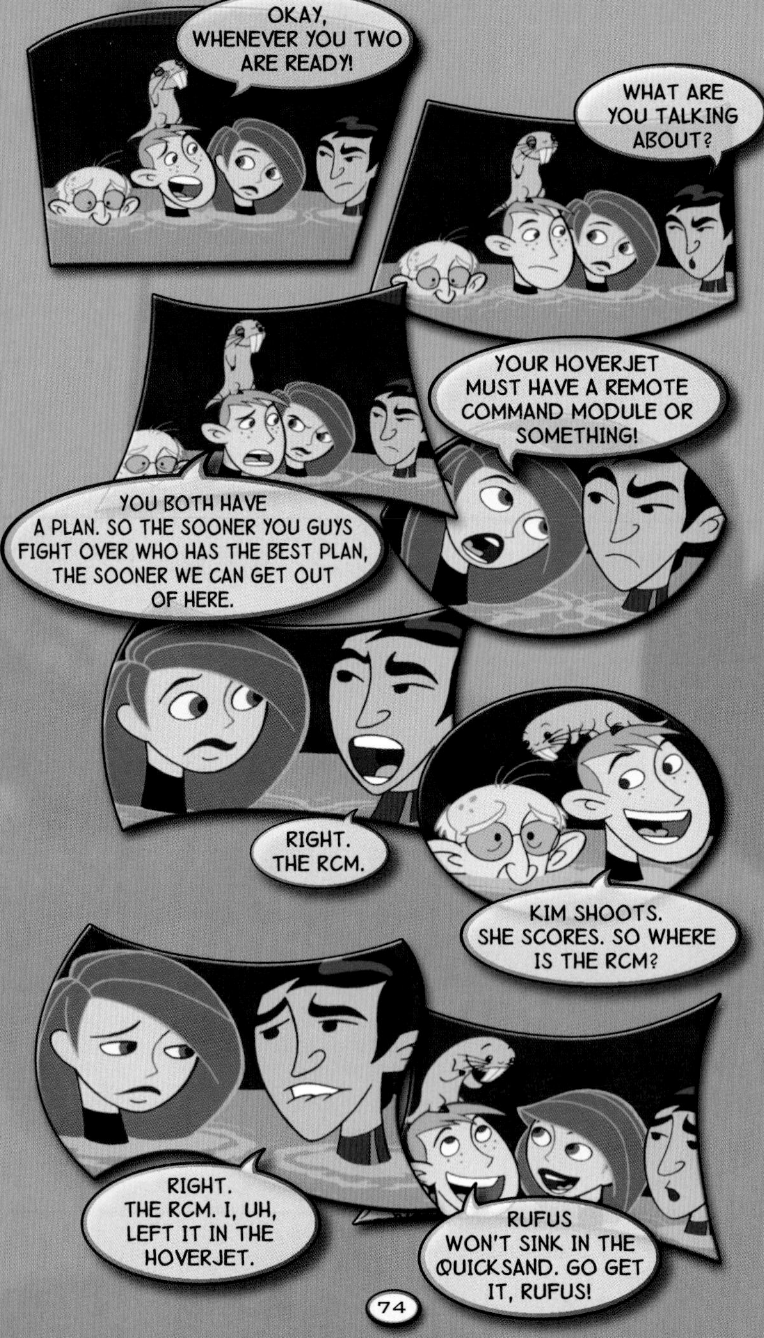
OKAY, WHENEVER YOU TWO ARE READY!
WHAT ARE YOU TALKING ABOUT?
YOUR HOVERJET MUST HAVE A REMOTE COMMAND MODULE OR SOMETHING!
YOU BOTH HAVE A PLAN. SO THE SOONER YOU GUYS FIGHT OVER WHO HAS THE BEST PLAN, THE SOONER WE CAN GET OUT OF HERE.
RIGHT. THE RCM.
KIM SHOOTS. SHE SCORES. SO WHERE IS THE RCM?
RIGHT. THE RCM. I, UH, LEFT IT IN THE HOVERJET.
RUFUS WON'T SINK IN THE QUICKSAND. GO GET IT, RUFUS!

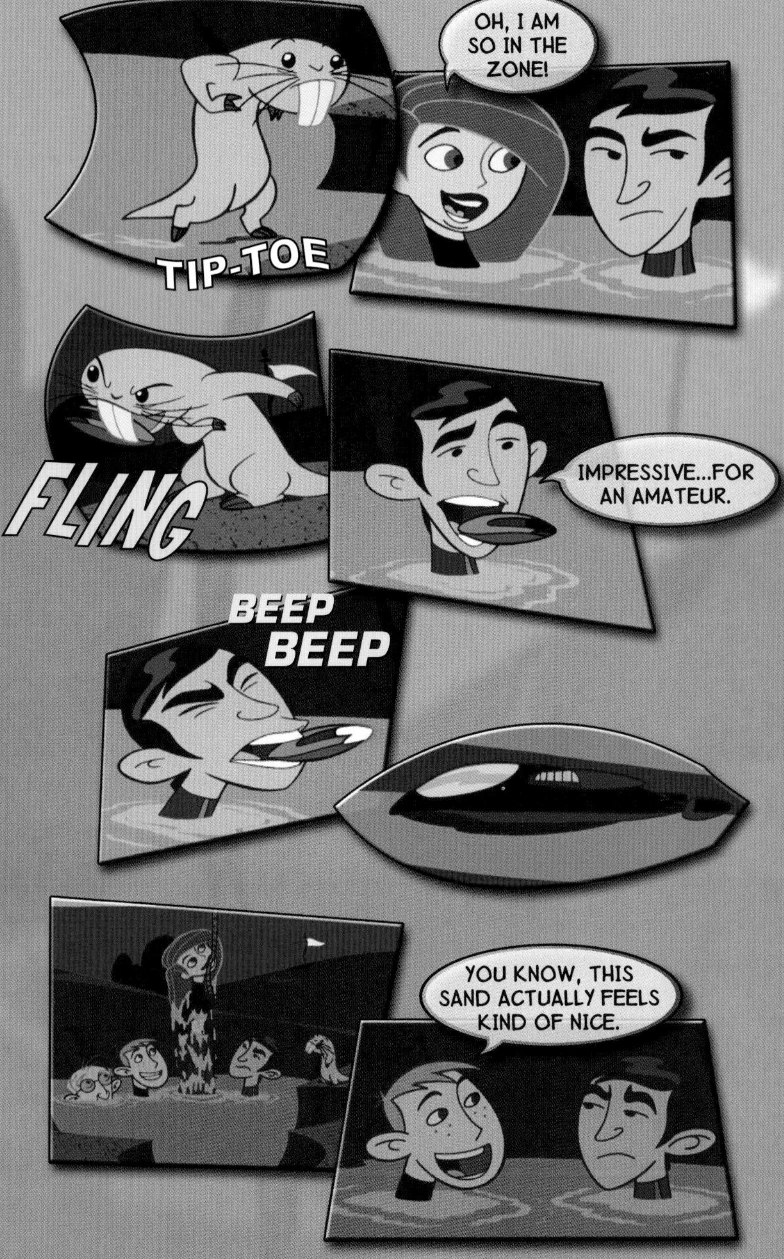
OH, I AM SO IN THE ZONE!
TIP-TOE
FLING
IMPRESSIVE...FOR AN AMATEUR.
BEEP BEEP
YOU KNOW, THIS SAND ACTUALLY FEELS KIND OF NICE.

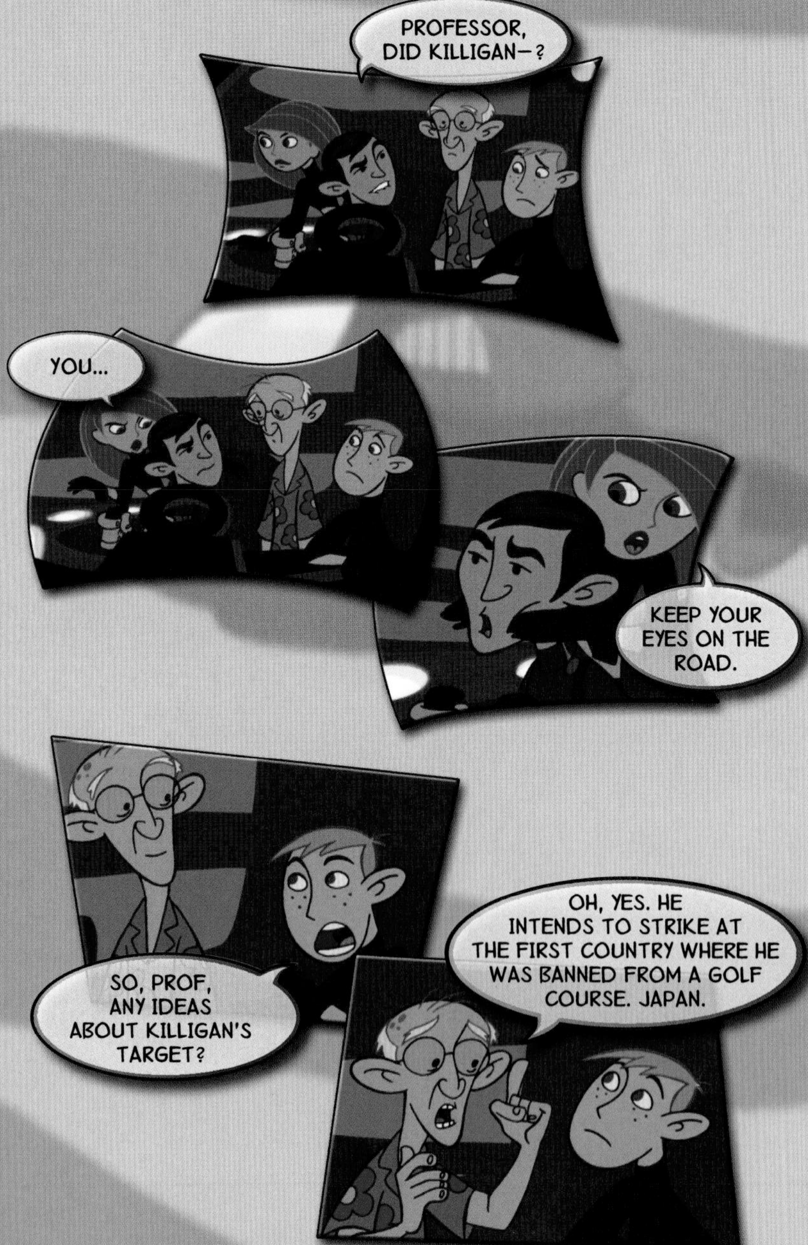
PROFESSOR, DID KILLIGAN—?
YOU...
KEEP YOUR EYES ON THE ROAD.
SO, PROF, ANY IDEAS ABOUT KILLIGAN'S TARGET?
OH, YES. HE INTENDS TO STRIKE AT THE FIRST COUNTRY WHERE HE WAS BANNED FROM A GOLF COURSE. JAPAN.

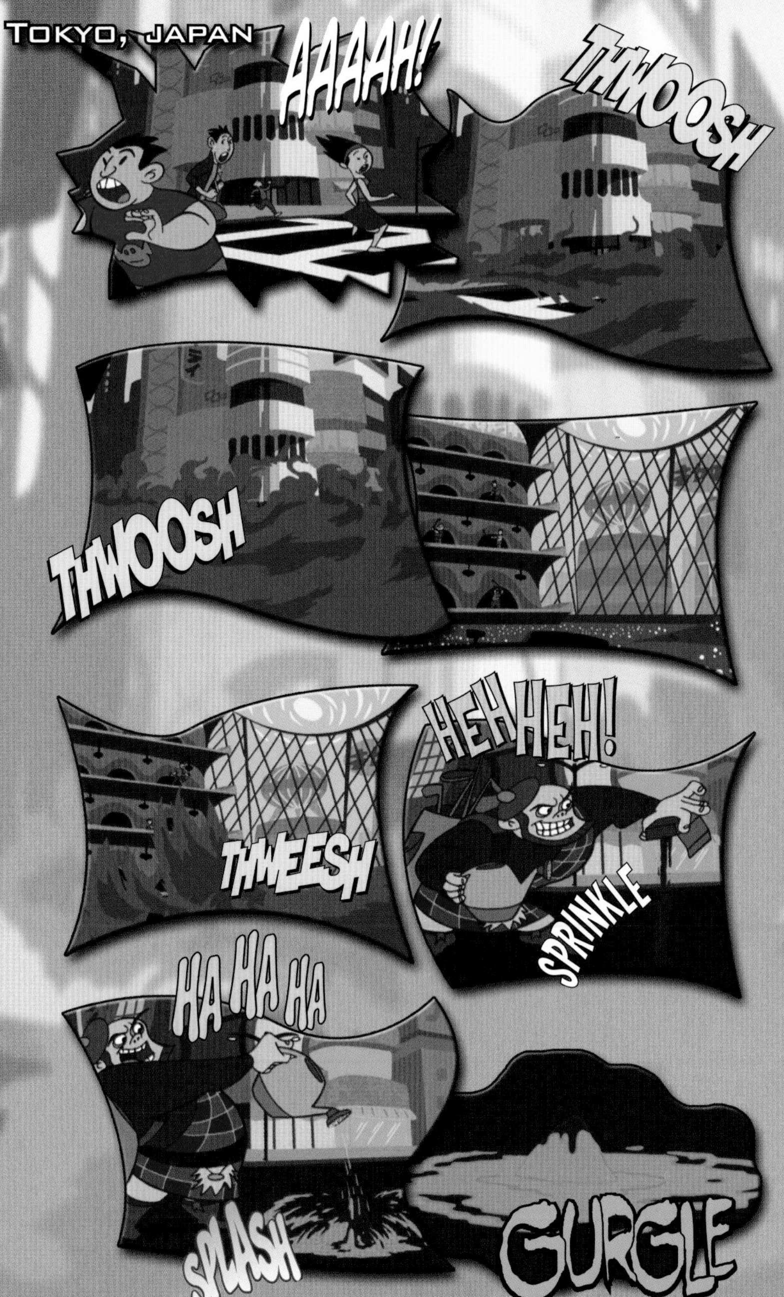
TOKYO, JAPAN
AAAAH!
THWOOSH
THWOOSH
THWEESH
HEH HEH!
SPRINKLE
HA HA HA
SPLASH
GURGLE

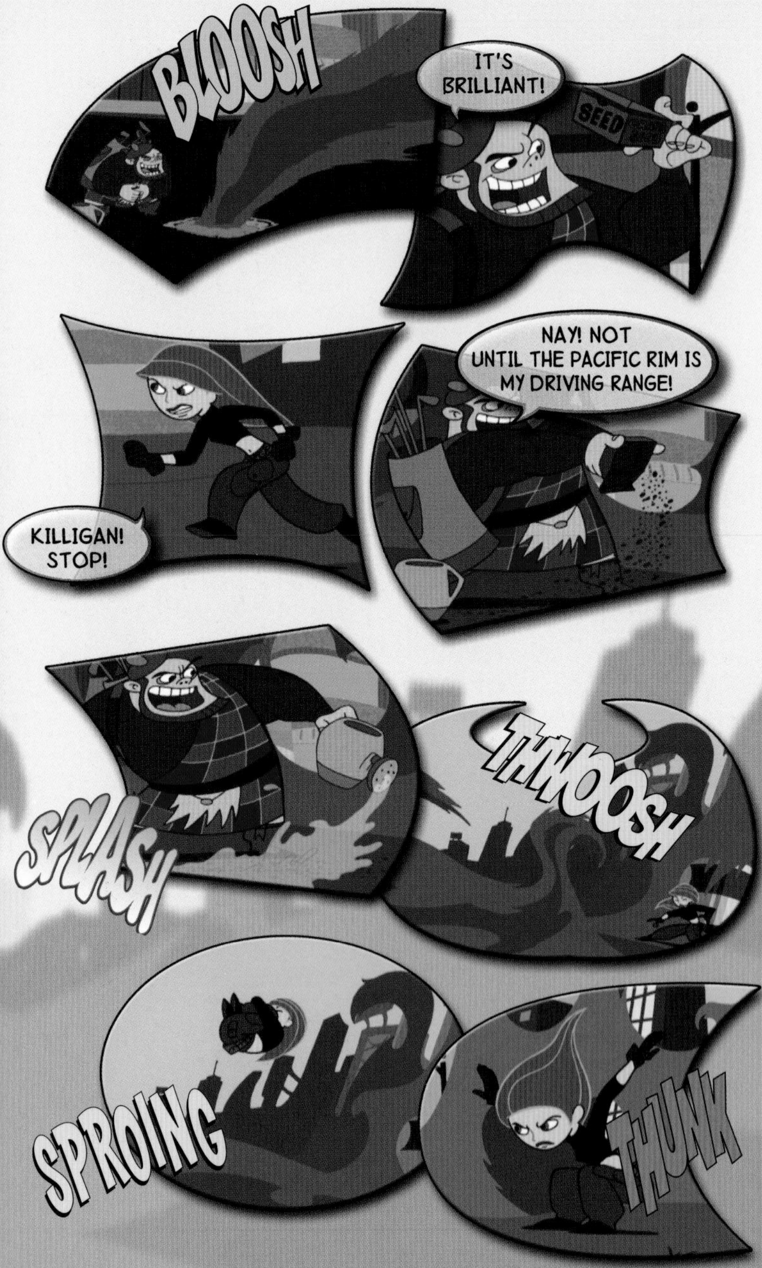
BLOOSH
IT'S BRILLIANT!
SEED
KILLIGAN! STOP!
NAY! NOT UNTIL THE PACIFIC RIM IS MY DRIVING RANGE!
SPLASH
THWOOSH
SPROING
THUNK

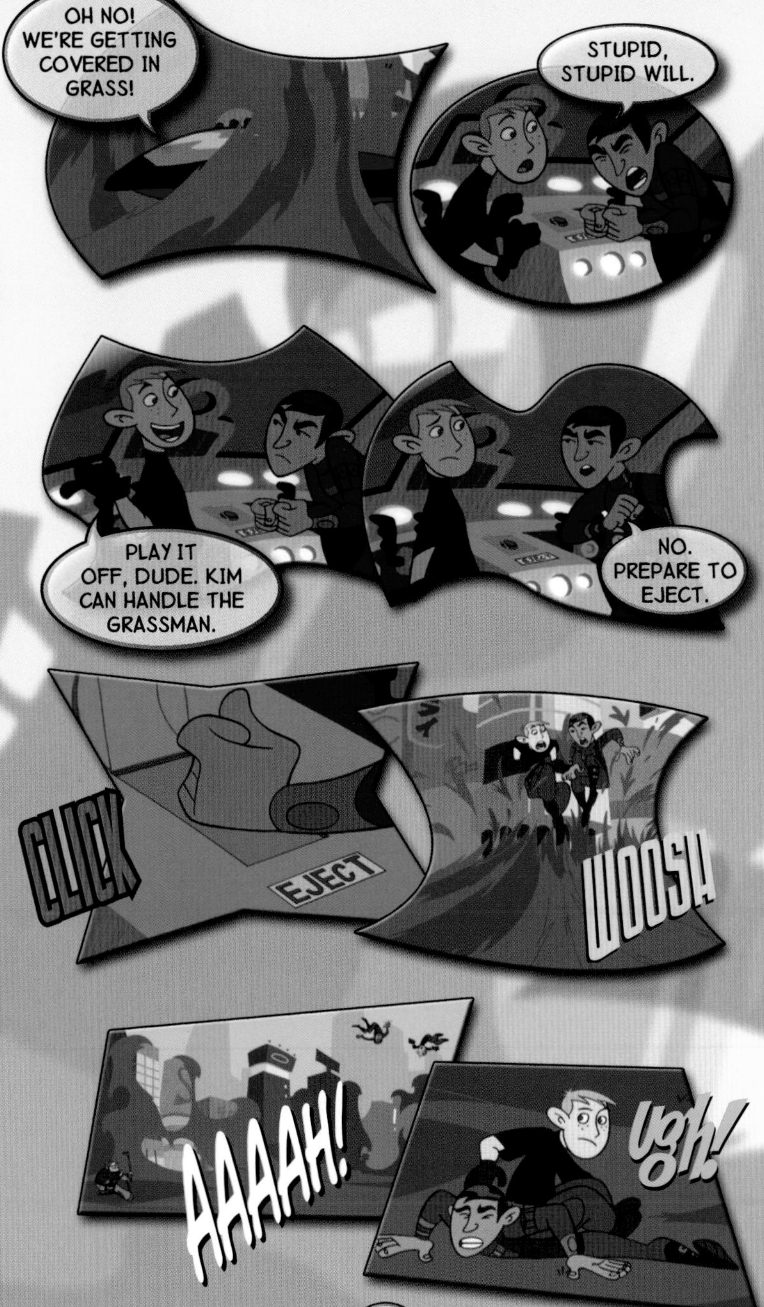
OH NO! WE'RE GETTING COVERED IN GRASS!
STUPID, STUPID WILL.
PLAY IT OFF, DUDE. KIM CAN HANDLE THE GRASSMAN.
NO. PREPARE TO EJECT.
CLICK
EJECT
WOOSH
AAAAH!
Ugh!

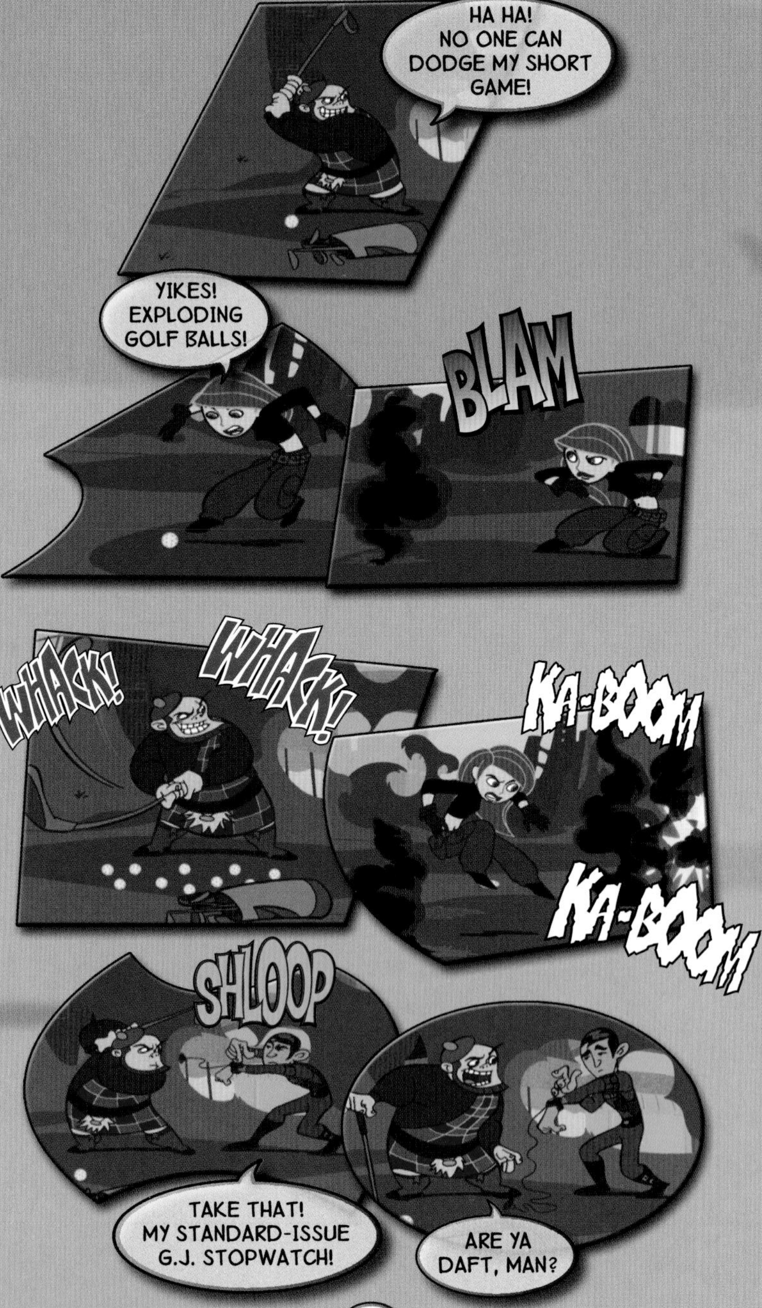
HA HA! NO ONE CAN DODGE MY SHORT GAME!
YIKES! EXPLODING GOLF BALLS!
BLAM
WHACK!
WHACK!
KA-BOOM
KA-BOOM
SHLOOP
TAKE THAT! MY STANDARD-ISSUE G.J. STOPWATCH!
ARE YA DAFT, MAN?

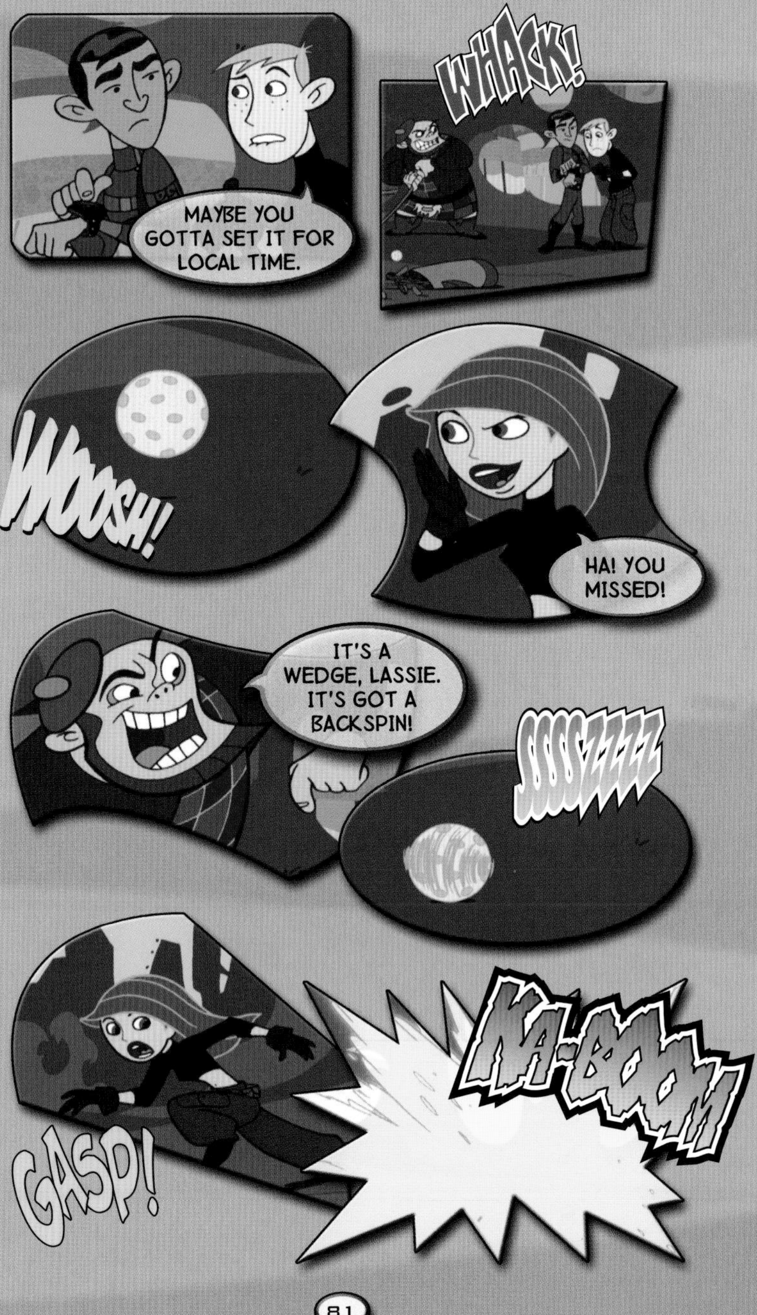
MAYBE YOU GOTTA SET IT FOR LOCAL TIME.
WHACK!
WOOSH!
HA! YOU MISSED!
IT'S A WEDGE, LASSIE. IT'S GOT A BACKSPIN!
SSSSZZZZZ
KA-BOOM
GASP!

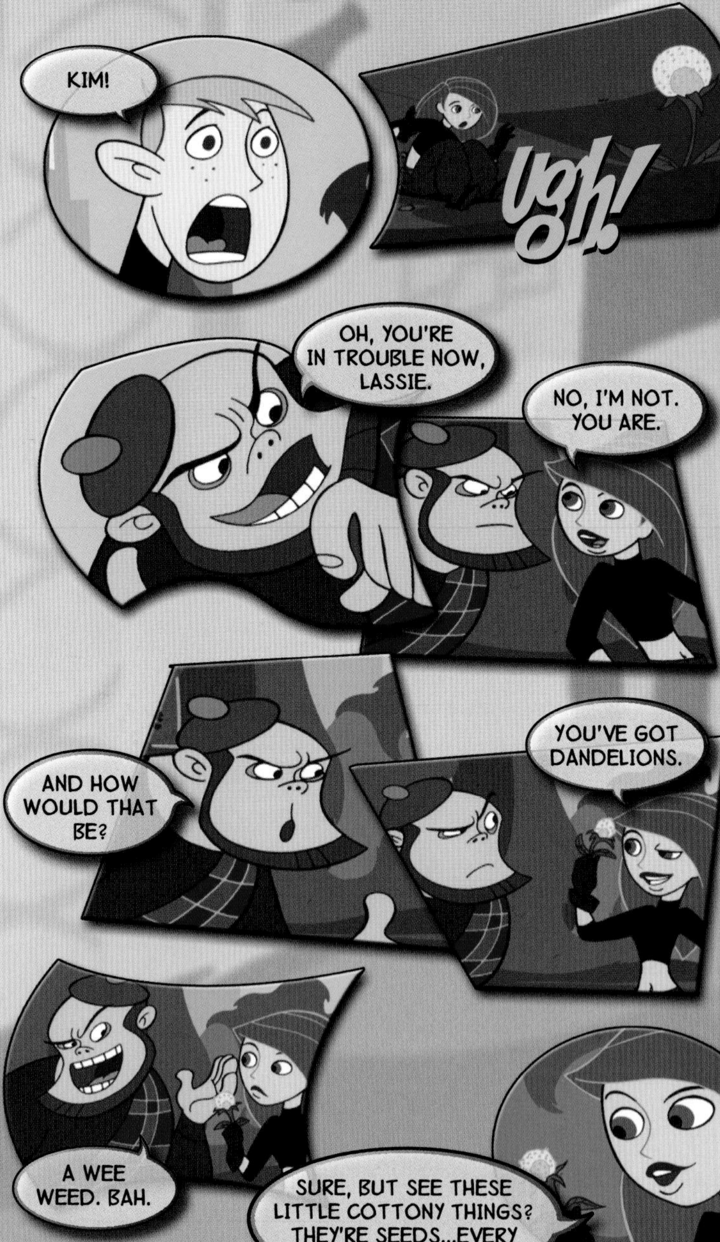
KIM!
Ugh!
OH, YOU'RE IN TROUBLE NOW, LASSIE.
NO, I'M NOT. YOU ARE.
AND HOW WOULD THAT BE?
YOU'VE GOT DANDELIONS.
A WEE WEED. BAH.
SURE, BUT SEE THESE LITTLE COTTONY THINGS? THEY'RE SEEDS...EVERY ONE OF THEM.

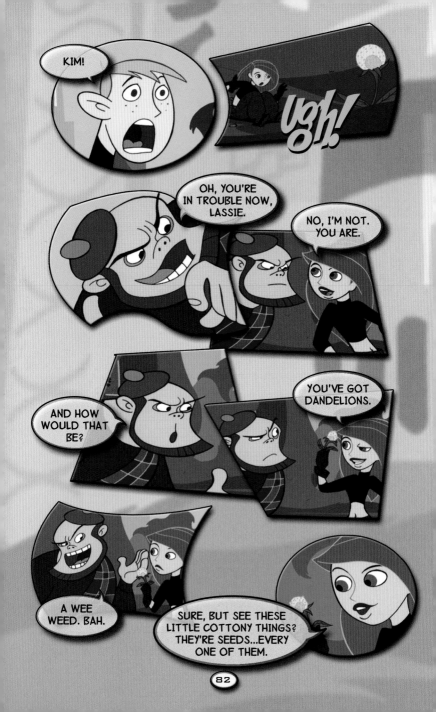

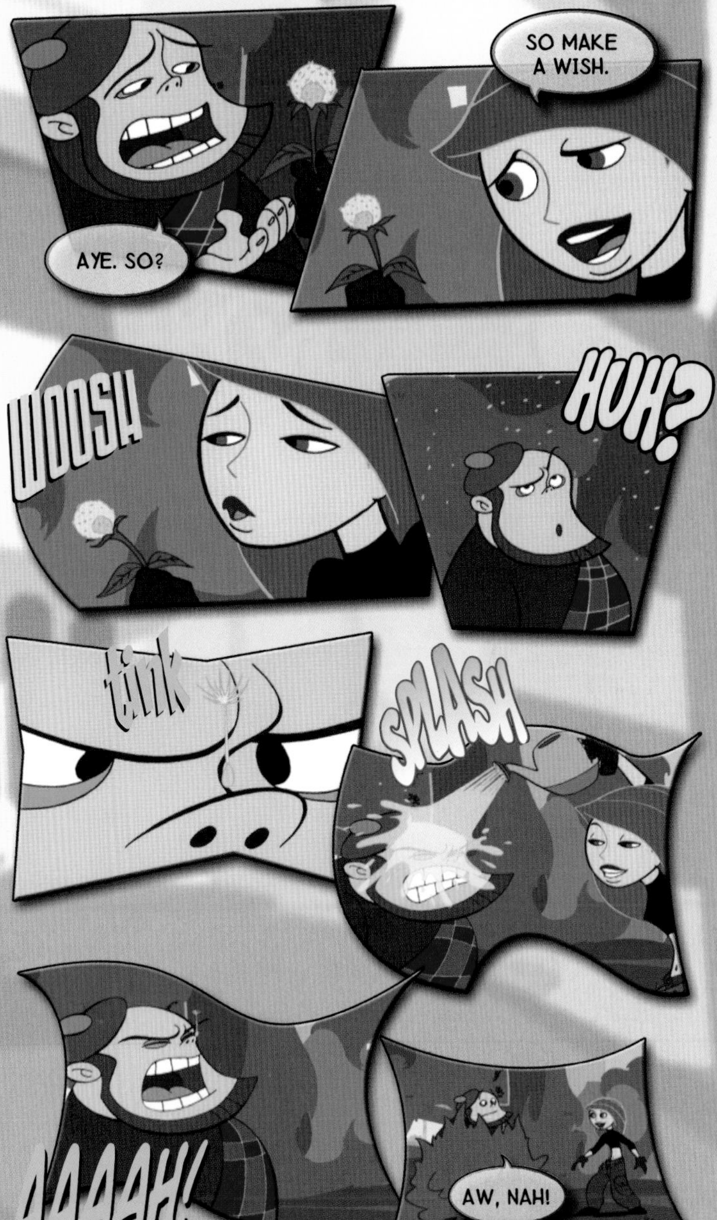
SO MAKE A WISH.
AYE. SO?
WOOSH
HUH?
tink
SPLASH
AAAAH!
AW, NAH!

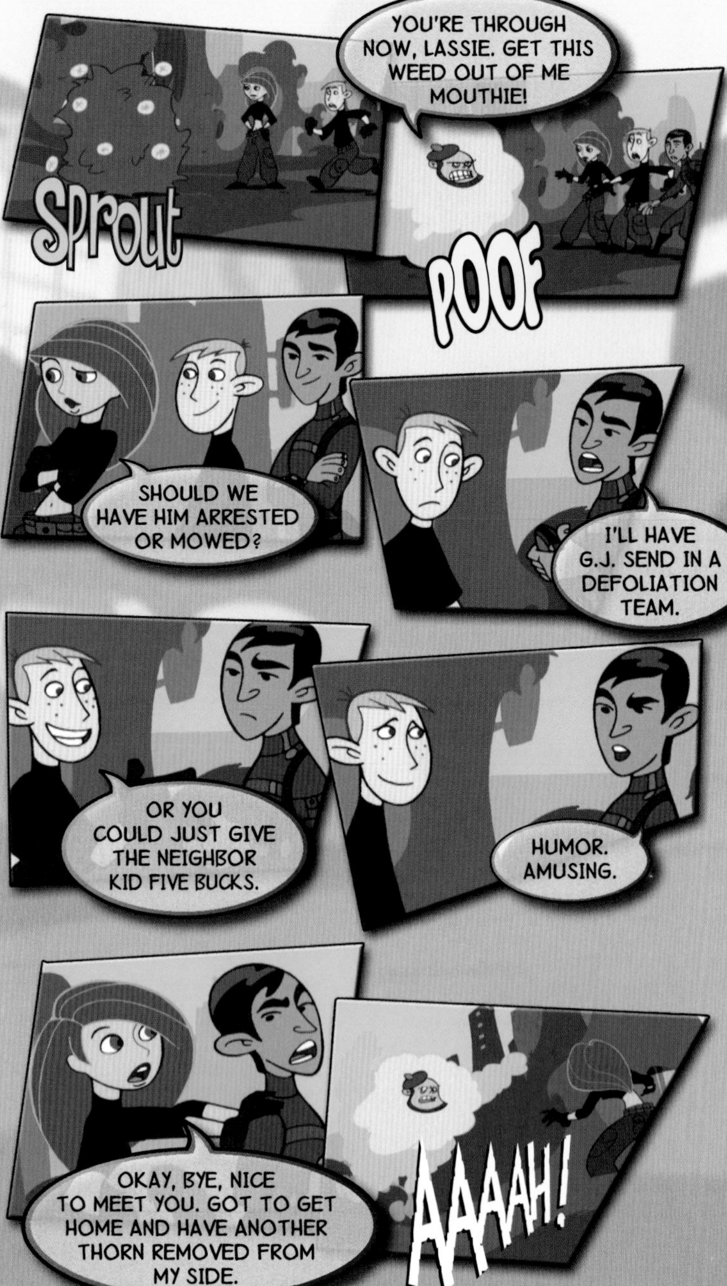
SPROUT
YOU'RE THROUGH NOW, LASSIE. GET THIS WEED OUT OF ME MOUTHIE!
POOF
SHOULD WE HAVE HIM ARRESTED OR MOWED?
I'LL HAVE G.J. SEND IN A DEFOLIATION TEAM.
OR YOU COULD JUST GIVE THE NEIGHBOR KID FIVE BUCKS.
HUMOR. AMUSING.
OKAY, BYE, NICE TO MEET YOU. GOT TO GET HOME AND HAVE ANOTHER THORN REMOVED FROM MY SIDE.
AAAAH!

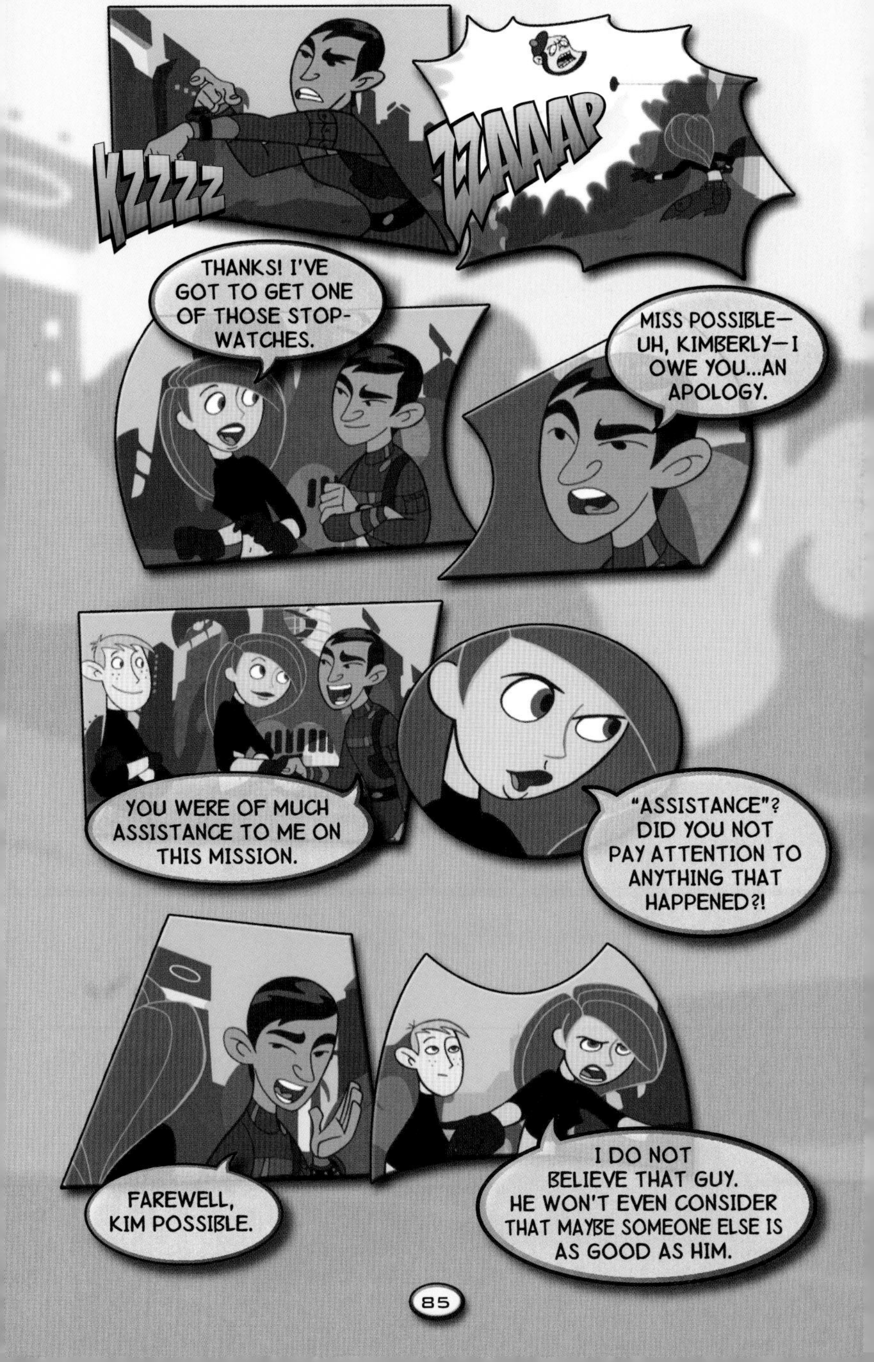
KZZZZ
ZZAAAP
THANKS! I'VE GOT TO GET ONE OF THOSE STOP-WATCHES.
MISS POSSIBLE—UH, KIMBERLY—I OWE YOU...AN APOLOGY.
YOU WERE OF MUCH ASSISTANCE TO ME ON THIS MISSION.
"ASSISTANCE"? DID YOU NOT PAY ATTENTION TO ANYTHING THAT HAPPENED?!
FAREWELL, KIM POSSIBLE.
I DO NOT BELIEVE THAT GUY. HE WON'T EVEN CONSIDER THAT MAYBE SOMEONE ELSE IS AS GOOD AS HIM.

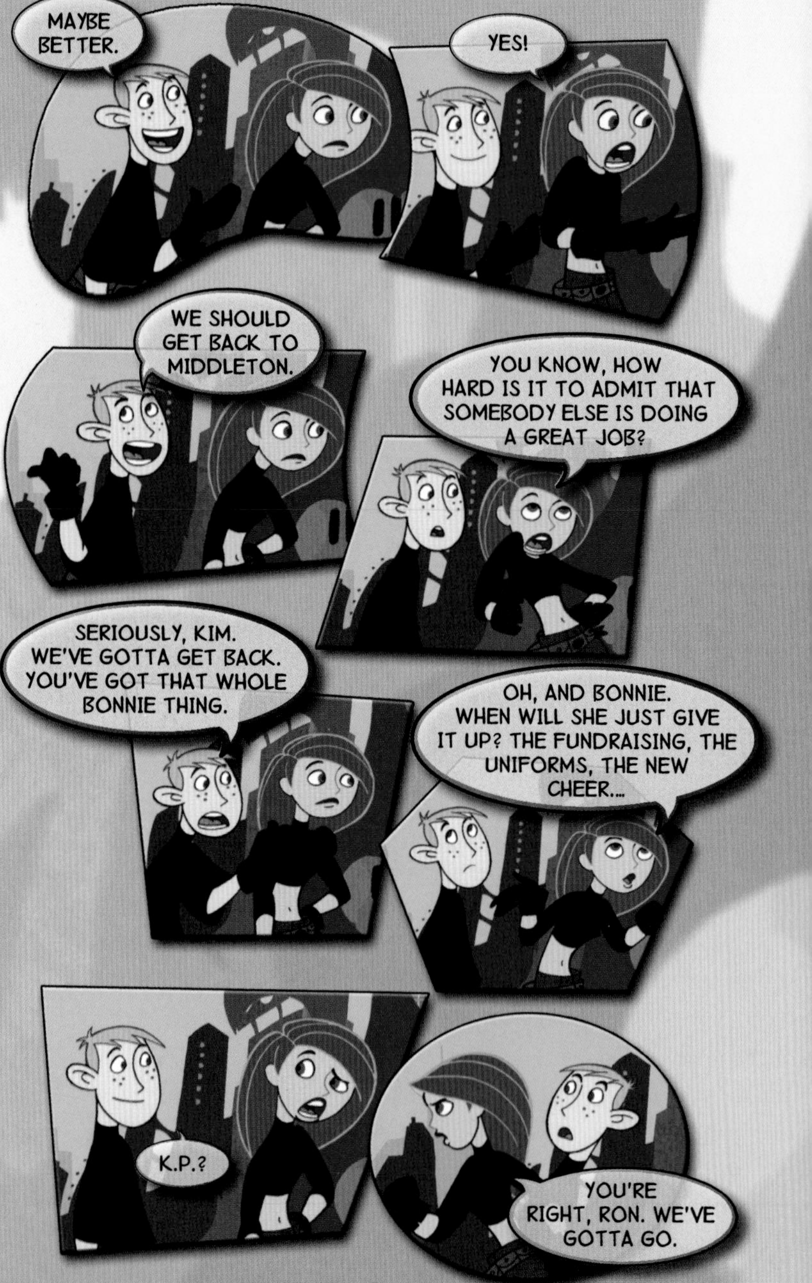
MAYBE BETTER.
YES!
WE SHOULD GET BACK TO MIDDLETON.
YOU KNOW, HOW HARD IS IT TO ADMIT THAT SOMEBODY ELSE IS DOING A GREAT JOB?
SERIOUSLY, KIM. WE'VE GOTTA GET BACK. YOU'VE GOT THAT WHOLE BONNIE THING.
OH, AND BONNIE. WHEN WILL SHE JUST GIVE IT UP? THE FUNDRAISING, THE UNIFORMS, THE NEW CHEER....
K.P.?
YOU'RE RIGHT, RON. WE'VE GOTTA GO.

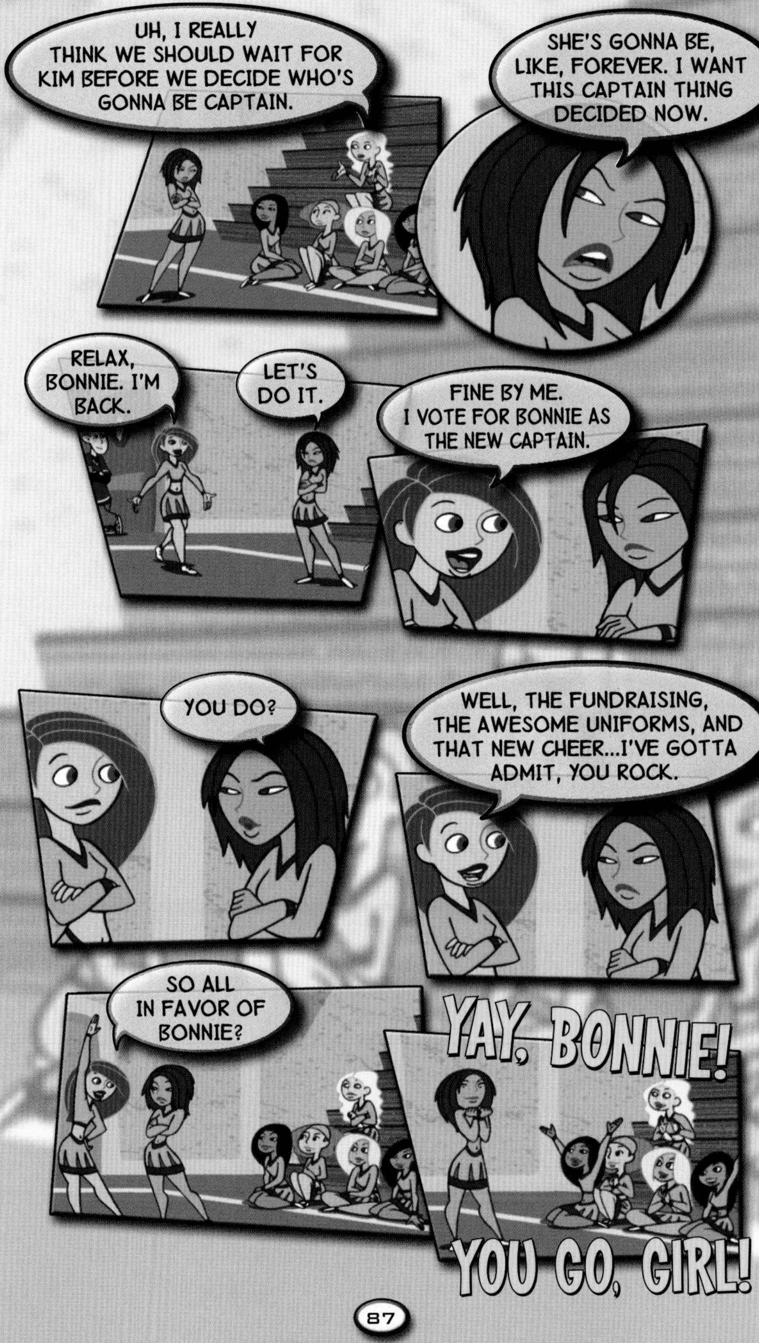
UH, I REALLY THINK WE SHOULD WAIT FOR KIM BEFORE WE DECIDE WHO'S GONNA BE CAPTAIN.
SHE'S GONNA BE, LIKE, FOREVER. I WANT THIS CAPTAIN THING DECIDED NOW.
RELAX, BONNIE. I'M BACK.
LET'S DO IT.
FINE BY ME. I VOTE FOR BONNIE AS THE NEW CAPTAIN.
YOU DO?
WELL, THE FUNDRAISING, THE AWESOME UNIFORMS, AND THAT NEW CHEER...I'VE GOTTA ADMIT, YOU ROCK.
SO ALL IN FAVOR OF BONNIE?
YAY, BONNIE!
YOU GO, GIRL!

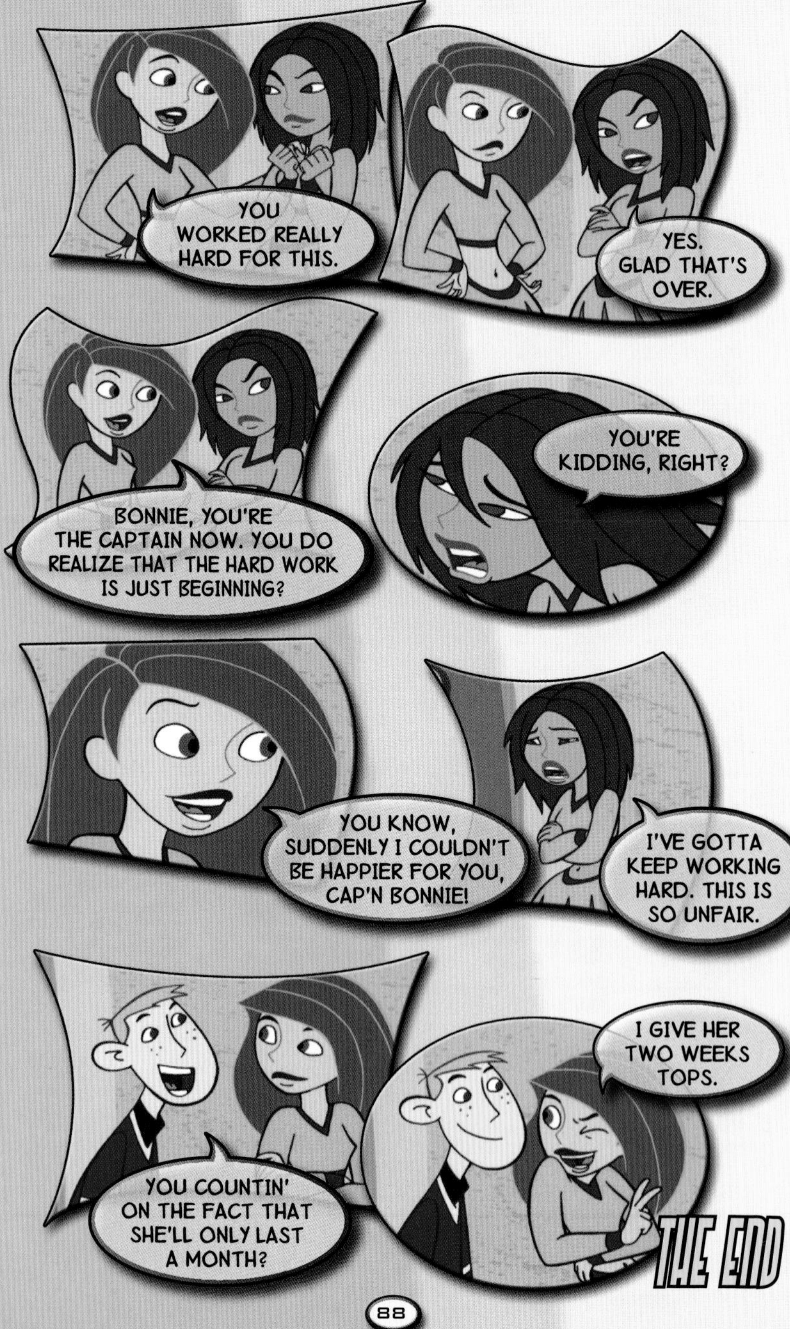
YOU WORKED REALLY HARD FOR THIS.
YES. GLAD THAT'S OVER.
BONNIE, YOU'RE THE CAPTAIN NOW. YOU DO REALIZE THAT THE HARD WORK IS JUST BEGINNING?
YOU'RE KIDDING, RIGHT?
YOU KNOW, SUDDENLY I COULDN'T BE HAPPIER FOR YOU, CAP'N BONNIE!
I'VE GOTTA KEEP WORKING HARD. THIS IS SO UNFAIR.
YOU COUNTIN' ON THE FACT THAT SHE'LL ONLY LAST A MONTH?
I GIVE HER TWO WEEKS TOPS.
THE END

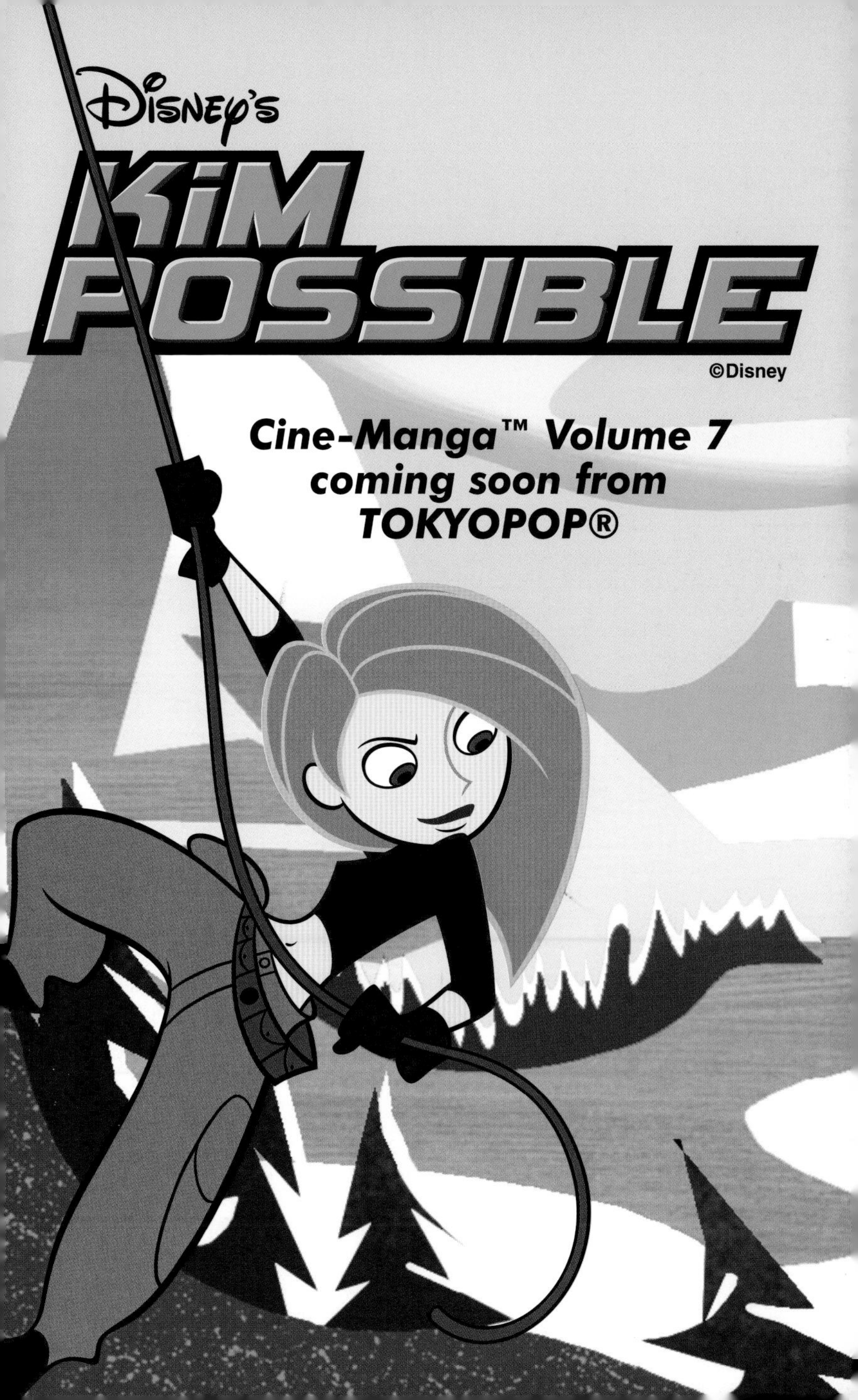
Disney's
Kim Possible
©Disney
Cine-Manga™ Volume 7
coming soon from
TOKYOPOP®

ALSO AVAILABLE FROM TOKYOPOP

MANGA

.HACK//LEGEND OF THE TWILIGHT
ANGELIC LAYER
BABY BIRTH
BRAIN POWERED
BRIGADOON
B'TX
CANDIDATE FOR GODDESS, THE
CARDCAPTOR SAKURA
CARDCAPTOR SAKURA - MASTER OF THE CLOW
CHRONICLES OF THE CURSED SWORD
CLAMP SCHOOL DETECTIVES
CLOVER
COMIC PARTY
CORRECTOR YUI
COWBOY BEBOP
COWBOY BEBOP: SHOOTING STAR
CRESCENT MOON
CULDCEPT
CYBORG 009
D.N. ANGEL
DEMON DIARY
DEMON ORORON, THE
DIGIMON
DIGIMON ZERO TWO
DIGIMON TAMERS
DRAGON HUNTER
DRAGON KNIGHTS
DREAM SAGA
DUKLYON: CLAMP SCHOOL DEFENDERS
ET CETERA
ETERNITY
FAERIES' LANDING
FLCL
FORBIDDEN DANCE
FRUITS BASKET
G GUNDAM
GATE KEEPERS
GIRL GOT GAME
GUNDAM SEED ASTRAY
GUNDAM WING
GUNDAM WING: BATTLEFIELD OF PACIFISTS
GUNDAM WING: ENDLESS WALTZ
GUNDAM WING: THE LAST OUTPOST (G-UNIT)
HARLEM BEAT
I.N.V.U.

INITIAL D
JING: KING OF BANDITS
JULINE
KARE KANO
KILL ME, KISS ME
KINDAICHI CASE FILES, THE
KING OF HELL
KODOCHA: SANA'S STAGE
LEGEND OF CHUN HYANG, THE
MAGIC KNIGHT RAYEARTH I
MAGIC KNIGHT RAYEARTH II
MAN OF MANY FACES
MARMALADE BOY
MARS
MINK
MIRACLE GIRLS
MODEL
ONE
PEACH GIRL
PEACH GIRL: CHANGE OF HEART
PITA-TEN
PLANET LADDER
PLANETES
PRINCESS AI
PSYCHIC ACADEMY
RAGNAROK
RAVE MASTER
REALITY CHECK
REBIRTH
REBOUND
RISING STARS OF MANGA
SAILOR MOON
SAINT TAIL
SAMURAI GIRL REAL BOUT HIGH SCHOOL
SEIKAI TRILOGY, THE CREST OF THE STARS
SGT. FROG
SHAOLIN SISTERS
SHIRAHIME-SYO: SNOW GODDESS TALES
SKULL MAN, THE
SUIKODEN III
SUKI
THREADS OF TIME
TOKYO MEW MEW
VAMPIRE GAME
WISH
WORLD OF HARTZ
ZODIAC P.I.

01.09.04Y

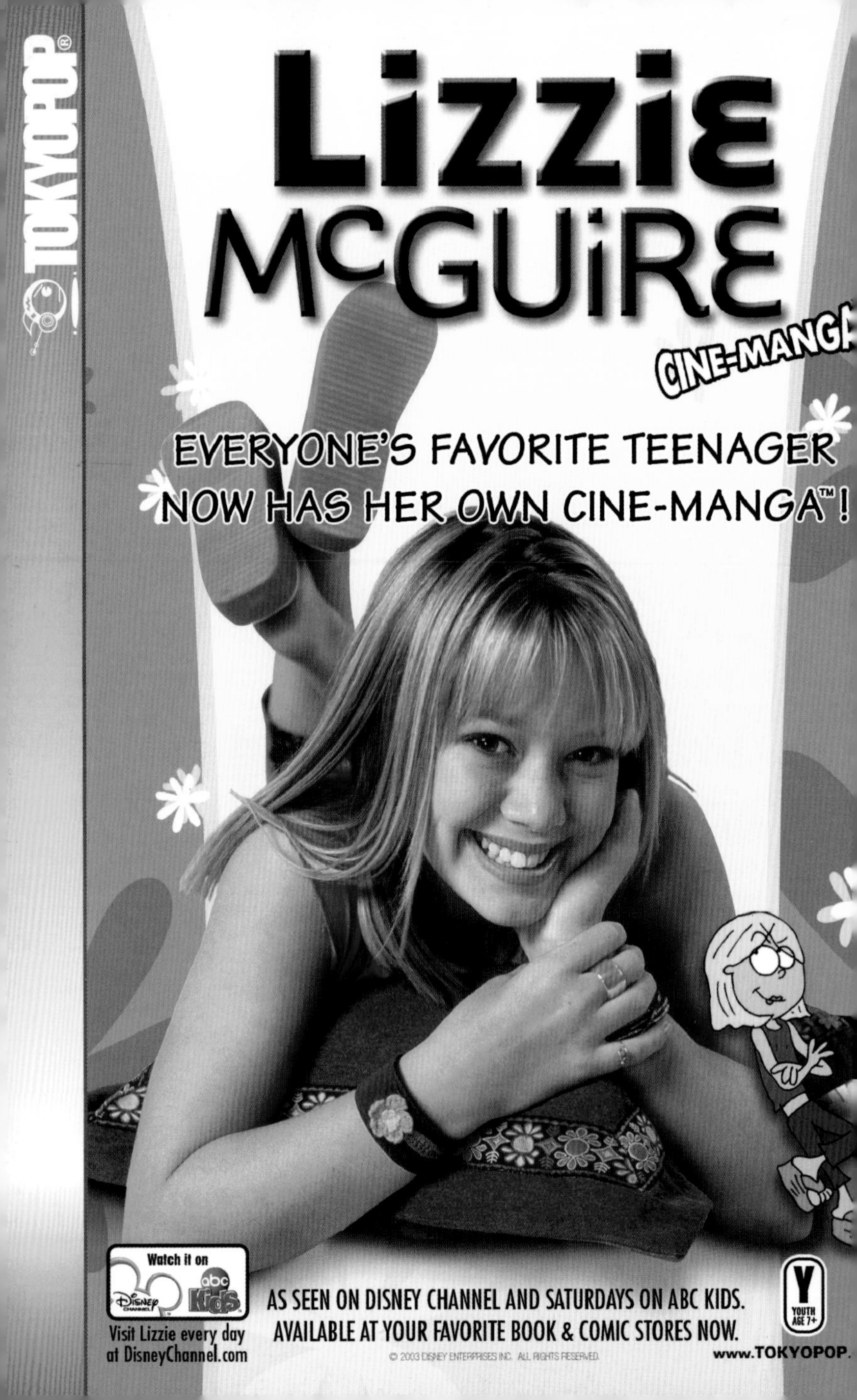
TOKYOPOP®
Lizzie McGUIRE
CINE-MANGA
EVERYONE'S FAVORITE TEENAGER NOW HAS HER OWN CINE-MANGA™!
Watch it on
DISNEY CHANNEL
abc Kids
Visit Lizzie every day at DisneyChannel.com
AS SEEN ON DISNEY CHANNEL AND SATURDAYS ON ABC KIDS.
AVAILABLE AT YOUR FAVORITE BOOK & COMIC STORES NOW.
© 2003 DISNEY ENTERPRISES INC. ALL RIGHTS RESERVED.
Y
YOUTH AGE 7+
www.TOKYOPOP.

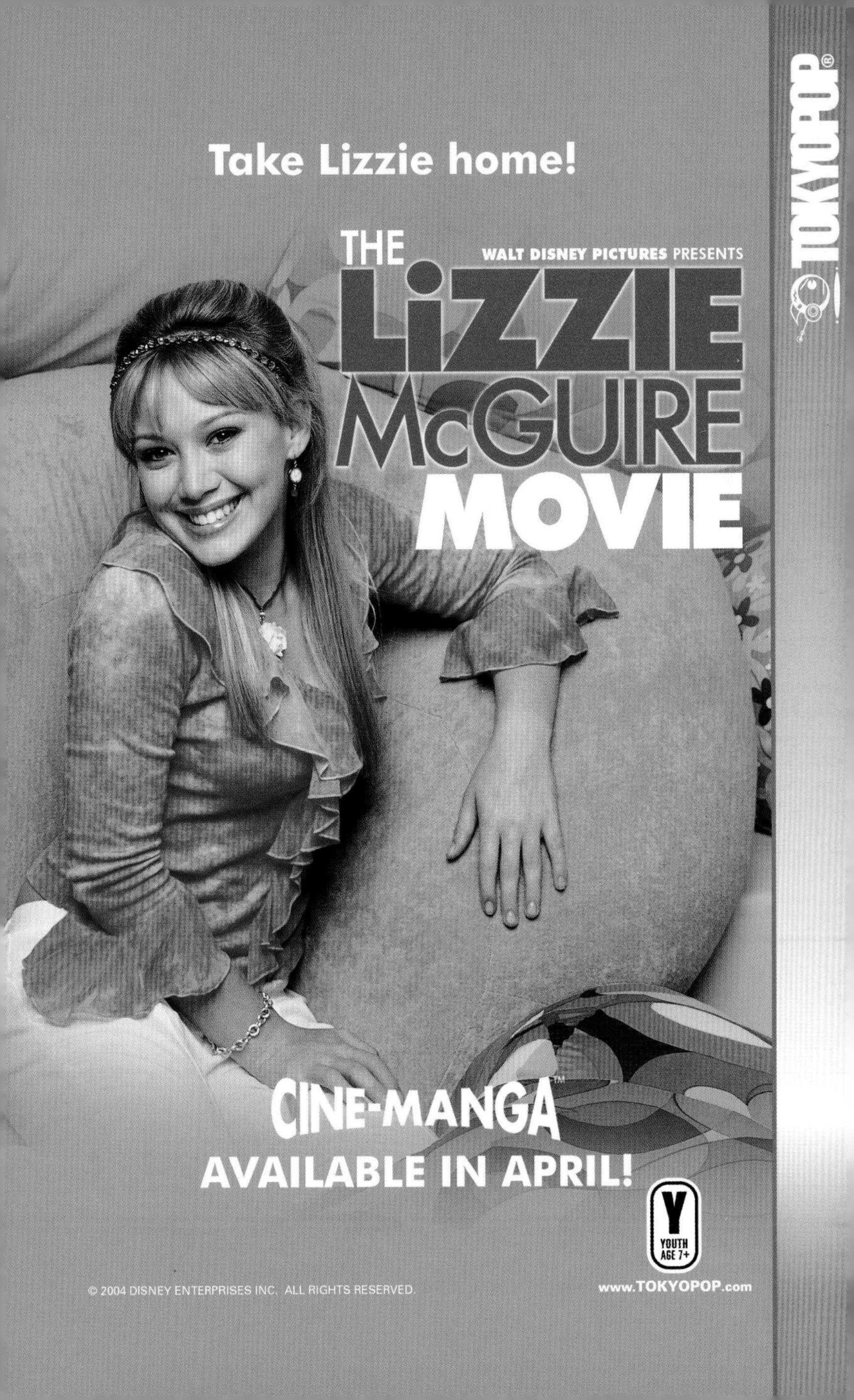
Take Lizzie home!
WALT DISNEY PICTURES PRESENTS
THE LIZZIE McGUIRE MOVIE
CINE-MANGA™
AVAILABLE IN APRIL!
Y YOUTH AGE 7+
© 2004 DISNEY ENTERPRISES INC. ALL RIGHTS RESERVED.
www.TOKYOPOP.com
TOKYOPOP®

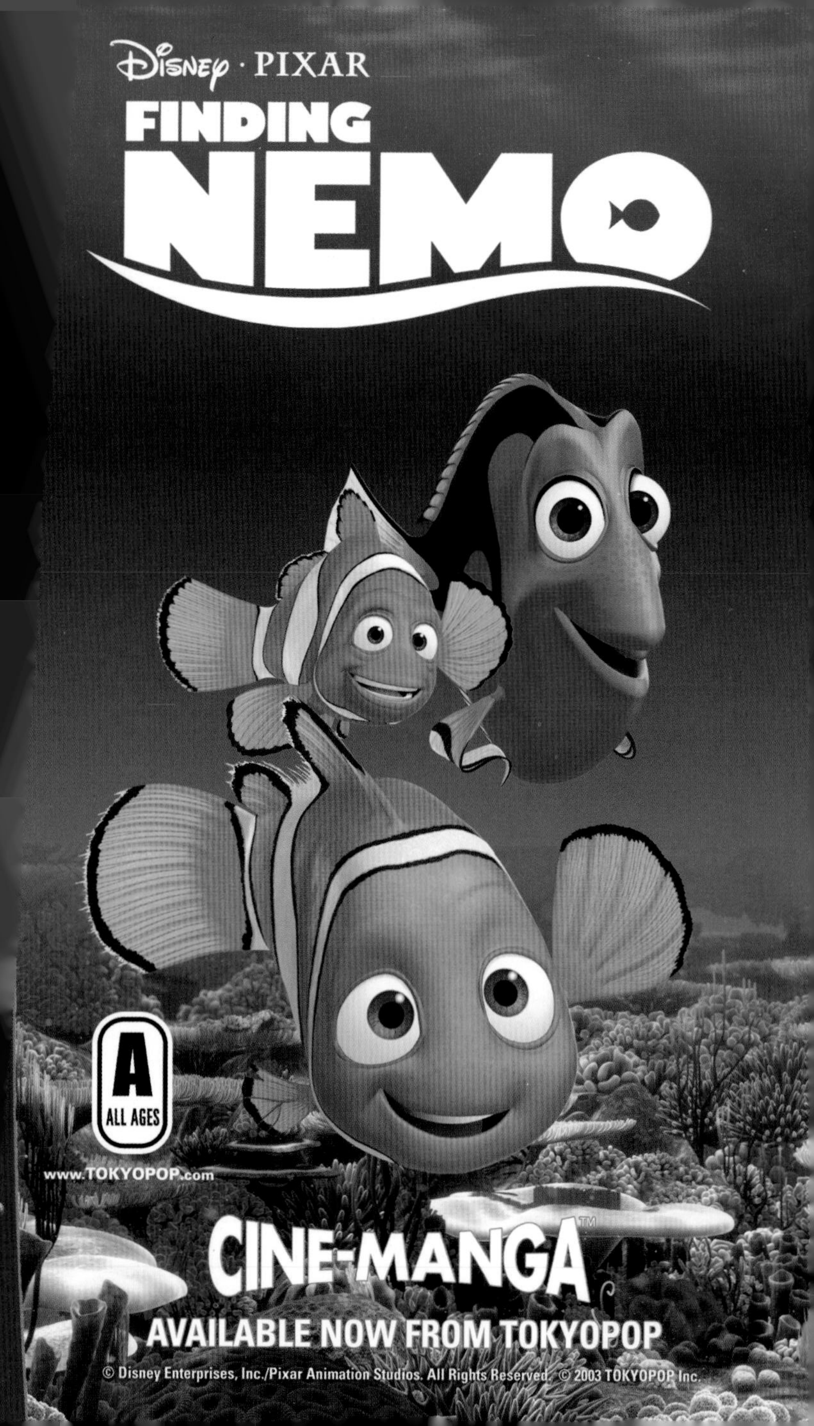
Disney · PIXAR
FINDING NEMO
A ALL AGES
www.TOKYOPOP.com
CINE-MANGA™
AVAILABLE NOW FROM TOKYOPOP
© Disney Enterprises, Inc./Pixar Animation Studios. All Rights Reserved. © 2003 TOKYOPOP Inc.